THROUGH TRAUMA TO GRACE

ISBN (Paperback): 979-8-9895820-0-6

ISBN (eBook): 979-8-9895820-1-3

THROUGH TRAUMA TO GRACE

Katrina Stewart

I dedicate this book to my Momma. Our stories were intertwined. I couldn't tell my story without sharing yours, Mom. Thank you for giving me permission to do so.

✝

A special dedication to my husband, and the love of my life, Darnell.
You've always believed I could achieve anything I set my mind to do. You are my biggest supporter.

To my children Domenique, Kortez, Camille, and Kennon, thank you for your encouragement and support while I labored through this book. Kennon, your edits brought the story over the finish line. Thank you, family, for believing in me.

✝

Sherry Pie, thank you for filling in the blanks of our family history. Your rich words helped me understand the truth, as hard as it was. Your strength encouraged me to stand.

To my Inner Circle, thank you. You ladies exemplify the characteristics of a true sisterhood. I reached out to you when I didn't want to move forward, and you helped me navigate the process through prayers, laughter, tears, and hope ... thank you!
You know who you are, and I honor you in this dedication.

✝

The healing that took place throughout the process of writing this book always drove me back to the Sovereignty and Mercy of God. I'm grateful God assigned me to be the one to reveal the truth, and shed the light of how I was delivered
Through Trauma to Grace.

Contents

God had a plan for my life, but I was unable to see it at the time. I was focused on my present state of living, trying to survive. Retreating into the closet, I felt as though I was invisible to the world. In the closet I could let all the pain surface, hot tears running down my face while my body would tremble from the uncontrollable silent sobs of hurtful agony.

In those dark, depressing hours in that closet, I learned to pray. Those scripture tracts the Bible Study Ladies gave us at school slowly became my lifeline to God. As a child, the formality of prayer was taught to me from Matthew 6: 9-13, the Lord's Prayer. Jesus told His disciples to "Pray like this" and that formula was what I used.

I wanted God to take away all the hurt and pain while in its place, give me a perfect life. Well, in that closet, my prayers seemed to go unheard, but I had no idea what God was up to …

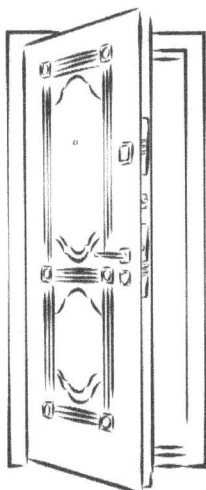

ONE

My grandmother, Claudia Walker, was born on December 4, 1924. Her parents, Dudley and Ida were two generations away from slavery, living in the small town of Vidilia, Louisiana. Claudia was very dark skinned like her father. The other children constantly teased her, calling her "Claude-of-dirt." Because of this, she adopted the nickname "Carrie." Carrie, later nicknamed, "Bigma," was one of six children living in a five-room hand-made home.

Her mother, my great-grandmother, Ida stayed at home while her father, (my great-grandfather), Dudley, worked as a sharecropper. Carrie's family and extended family were very close as most families were in the south. Momma Ida, as she was fondly called, was a praying woman who believed in God. She took good care of her husband, children, and grandchildren as well as any family that lived nearby. Momma Ida's beauty, shapely figure and big pretty legs were legendary. But she was most known for her praying spirit.

Momma Ida not only did the cleaning and cooking, but she would help her husband, Poppa Dudley, with hunting or anything else to provide for the family. Poppa was a hard worker but also one who was known for drinking and fighting. His moments of anger were explosive. The only time Momma Ida got angry was to bring Poppa under control. From what I could gather from stories from my grandmother Carrie, and conversations with my mom and her cousin Sherry, Momma Ida was loved by her children and grandchildren. The family loved hard and fought harder.

Food, alcohol, storytelling, and family gatherings were the elements of family bonding. There were times my first cousins and I sat around our older family members mesmerized! The oral history of our ancestors' lives growing up in the south was captivating and oftentimes mystical. Some of those tales of how our grandparents and great-grandparents lived were funny and enjoyable, yet there were other stories that scared the pants off us! Living in the south was a hard life for Black folks, so it made me appreciate the accomplishments of my grandmother Carrie and other elders. Mixed with love and appreciation was trepidation, however. There was a very dark side to their lives that generationally caused much pain. Spiritually speaking, the family followed a mixture of church going and voodoo spiritism. It is very difficult to reconcile these two ways of life.

Carrie resembled her mother Ida a lot with her shapely figure, big pretty legs, and flirtatious stride. She had dark skin that was incredibly smooth. Her sister, (my great-aunt), Annie, who was eighteen years older, was not known to be as physically attractive as her younger sister. Annie also possessed dark skin but was smaller in her body frame with wide hips. The left side of her face was slightly distorted, and her left eye was completely shut. It was said as a child, Annie was beating a snake with a stick and venom shot into her eye. It was a miracle she was still alive.

Eventually, Annie moved on her own and was living in a house near a railroad stop. It was a busy junction for soldiers and sharecroppers looking for work. Annie's house was where anyone could come to buy moonshine and sex. I recall being told that Carrie was sent to stay with Annie for a time. That's when she was introduced to this world of transients, liquor, and prostitution. I'm not sure how old Carrie was or how long this went on. I can only imagine that this was quite traumatizing to my grandmother Carrie, but in those days you dealt with life and kept moving. There was no time for sympathy; you learned to deal with life as it was and made the best of it. Abuse, trauma, and toxicity was a part of life because it was deep rooted from the many years of dehumanization because of slavery. Black people had to learn how to survive with the bare minimum of life's essentials in hopes of making life just a little easier. Unwanted pregnancies were also dealt with swiftly. Someone in the family would take the child as an undocumented adoption, the child would be left where it wouldn't be found, or the pregnancy was ended before the birth. Carrie and Annie made a living this way by performing backroom abortions.

Many stories were shared about Carrie's upbringing which explained the foundation of her hardness. She would speak of her past with a sense of pride and pain because it was a difficult life she arose from.

At the age of sixteen, Carrie became pregnant with her first child, who would be my aunt, Vera Mae. Matthew Rutland Sr., was Vera Mae's father and my grandfather. Family lore is that Annie's son, "Doughboy," told Matthew that Carrie was asking for cornmeal and milk. I guess telling Matthew about Carrie's cravings was his way of telling Matthew that Carrie was carrying his child. They both lived in a very small town where everyone knew everybody, but we don't know much about their courtship, or if there was any. My grandfather Matthew was six years older than Carrie and was from a deeply religious family with fourteen children. I believe, in part, that was why he married her and built a small two-room home for their family. He was a sharecropper, like his dad, and was determined to provide for his family. A year later in 1941, they had another child, my uncle, Matthew Rutland, Jr.

At this point, Matthew Sr., started looking for work in Michigan and was also studying for the ministry. He moved to Detroit and lived with family members until he found work. Carrie stayed close with her immediate family in Louisiana while he was gone, and this provided the family connections for them. Once granddad Matthew secured employment, he sent for Carrie and the two children. Some of granddad's siblings had also begun moving north, settling in

Michigan and Ohio, as many southern Black families did during "The Great Migration." This marked the beginning of a new chapter in both of their lives.

Getting to know my family's history was so important to me as a teenager. It gave me a sense of belonging and pride. My grandfather's side of the family always seemed "well put together, stern and religious." As they moved from the South, got married, and started families, they spoke less of the hard times from their childhood. They lived structured, highly religious lifestyles and did very well for themselves—owning businesses, sending their children to college, and owning their own homes. This was the ideal outcome for a Black family looking for a better life.

Yet, finding out the secrets of their past made them more human in my eyes, especially as we were judged so harshly by our elders—including Bigma, (my grandmother, Carrie), as if they never made any mistakes. These secrets also explained a lot of the whys behind their character.

My paternal grandmother, Ruby on the left. My
paternal grandfather Clyde, in the middle.
And Carrie, "Bigma" my maternal grandmother, on
the right.

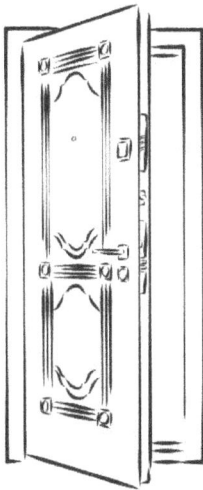

TWO

Aunt Annie moved to Michigan and bought a two family flat on the east side of Detroit where she lived with her common law husband, affectionately known as Papa Lowe. She began using Lowe as a last name, dropping Walker. She rented the upper flat to Carrie and Matthew when they moved their growing family to Detroit. The flat was a small two-bedroom home, but it was a good place to start.

In 1943, Carrie was pregnant again with their third child, Katie Bee, who died of what they believed was "crib death" or Sudden Infant Death in 1944.

Carrie would often speak of Katie coming to visit her at night, lying across her feet. Carrie's generation strongly believed in spirits, good and bad, and often reported seeing spirits walking around. She would say, there would be a heaviness laying across her feet and she would talk to Katie Bee.

Three years later, Carrie was pregnant with my mother, Lois Jean. Matthew, my Granddad, later shared with my mom that he had to fight with Carrie for her to carry the baby to term. She and Aunt Annie tried to abort the baby and when Granddad found out about it, he prayerfully found an old Jewish doctor who made house calls. The doctor provided prenatal care and put Carrie on total bed rest until she delivered my mom. Granddad was working full-time, had a pregnant wife and two children at home, ages six and seven. He did as much as he could, cooking, and taking care of the children while working full-time. They relied heavily on family to assist and he made sure to compensate them for their efforts as well as handle all the bills including the house calls made by the doctor.

Needless to say, when my mother Lois Jean was born, Carrie wasn't thrilled, but made the best of it. She would often tell my mom how much she hated Granddad for making her endure those months in bed for the sake of the pregnancy. My mom recalled how those statements made her feel unwanted as a daughter. Yet, knowing that her dad fought for her, made up for it to a small extent. Sometimes I would think about the relationship between a mother and her unborn child, and the bonding that takes place during the pregnancy. It would leave me wondering if the lack of a healthy attachment resulted in their dysfunctional mother-daughter relationship.

When my mom was old enough, Carrie began to work, and the family moved into their own home on the west side of Detroit. They attended St. Mark's Baptist Church where Granddad was ordained as a deacon and later studied to become an ordained minister. Carrie served in the Nurses' Guild. There are pictures of her with the Guild ladies, dressed to the nines in their white nurse's uniform and black shawls. Uniformity was extremely important with the ministries and without fail, she outshined them all.

But Carrie was not ready to become a preacher's wife. I can only imagine the struggles she faced between her painful past and damaging choices, the tumultuous family history, and then the strong push from her husband to be his upstanding wife. Separating herself from the partying and drinking to fully serve the church was not what she had in mind. Carrie loved that upbeat life. Living the life in the ministry was a blessing and curse to Carrie.

Carrie's mom, Momma Ida, was not described as a very domineering woman, but Carrie and the other women in the family were controlling. The women often overruled their husband's opinions. Carrie became a very manipulative and calculating woman. Maybe this had a lot to do with her desire to not be under a man's rule. Whatever the reason, Carrie went down a path many of the other women in the family had not done, by choosing to betray her marriage covenant to Matthew.

As I was writing this part of the book, I began to think of my own experience of feeling lonely in a marriage and needing the support of my husband. I considered the conflict between the desire to be his wife and to make him happy, yet at the same time not being happy within myself. Thinking that my husband would be the source of my happiness actually was the source of a lot of pain. Now I can see why or maybe understand what was happening in their marriage at this point. They were normal people trying to make the best of the situation they lived in, and when trouble arose in their marriage, they took what was probably the most convenient way out. The difference was that the other women stayed married. Carrie asked Matthew to leave.

My mom was somewhere between five and six years old when this happened. Carrie allowed another man to move in their home for a while. Then around the age of eight or nine, my mom was told by Carrie to tell her dad it was time for him to come home. But by this time, he had married another woman and was preparing to be ordained a minister of the Baptist faith. Granddad would often tell us how he didn't want to get a divorce, but Carrie had divorced him and by the time she was ready to reconcile, he had married another woman in the church who was widowed with three children. Up until this point, there was no mention in the family history of any couple getting a divorce. They may not have lived together, but they didn't end the marriage, they just figured out how to make it work. This cycle of divorce would run through the next generation like a curse, and that was exactly what the enemy wanted.

The only picture of little Lois Jean and her daddy.

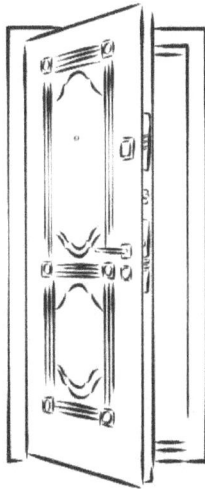

THREE

Carrie was a hard woman to love but she believed in taking care of her family and making sure no one was ever without. Despite being single, she raised her three children and a niece (from a sister who passed away) on her own until her kids were old enough to get jobs. Carrie had no problem keeping male companions, even though they were often abusive. She remained in the relationships until she had had enough and physically had to fight to put them out.

In order to make sure she could take care of herself and her family, she worked full time as a housekeeper in a nursing home or as a ladies room attendant on the Bob-Lo Boat; a ferry that took people to the Bob-Lo Amusement Park on an island in the Detroit river. But she soon reverted to her old lifestyle to make ends meet. Prostitution, liquor parties, and illegal abortions were the side hustle she and many of her friends made to keep the bills paid. Women "in the business" often taught these "trades" to their daughters. I'm not sure if Carrie taught these things to my aunt Vera, but I know that this was taught to my mom.

My mom told me about a time when she was around nine years old, and Carrie said that one of her boyfriends was going to buy my mom school clothes. My mom was really excited. She said she knew exactly what skirts, blouses, and shoes she would pick out because she loved to wear pleated skirts and ruffled front blouses. Having an older sister meant she wore a lot of hand-me-down clothes, so this was a chance for her to get some things of her own. That excitement soon faded when she was told by Carrie that she had to compensate him for it. No one questioned Carrie, she ruled with a heavy fist, a frying pan, and a small pistol— whichever she could get her hands on first. At the age of nine, my mom knew not to disobey when she was told to go into the black Cadillac parked behind the back of the house, and to do exactly what the guy requested. Once it was over, without a blink, Carrie told my mom to go wash up and never speak of it to anyone else. My mom knew the rules about what happened in the house. *What happened in the house, stayed in the house.* That was the beginning of their life as mother and daughter that defined their relationship and their positions in each other's lives.

The thing that stood out in Momma's and Carrie's relationship was Momma's desire to please her mother. Momma loved her mother so much and only wanted her mother's love in return, as any daughter would. But it was a love that Carrie was unable to show in the way Momma needed it. Both were dealing with their own demons.

A few years passed when Momma's sister got married and began having children. The children lovingly nicknamed Carrie, Bigma. The name stuck and Carrie was known as Bigma or Ms. Carrie— depending on your relationship with her.

Bigma's relationships with all her children were very dysfunctional to the point that it became physical between her and her daughters. Soon after the "incident" in the car, Momma began to sneak into Bigma's liquor stash. It helped to numb the emotional pain because it wasn't the only time it would happen. Unfortunately, she had no one to talk to about this and it stayed unspoken. Momma told me that she and her siblings were close mainly because of the abuse in the home towards her and her sister. Their brother Matthew tried to protect them, but he too couldn't stand up against Bigma. I'm sure he didn't want to physically hurt his mother, but children were also taught not to disrespect their parents. Matthew began working at the local phone company as a co-op student at the local high school. He used that money to buy Momma's school clothes and give her money to take care of herself. Momma learned how to stay out of the way of Bigma and take care of herself as much as possible. School became her safe place, and she was a very good student.

School is where Momma met my dad, Henry McIntosh. He attended another local high school and played on their football team. He showed Momma the attention and love she desired but was older than her by a few years. They began seeing each other under the watchful eye of Bigma but soon began to sneak around. Momma's first cousin Sherry had come to live with them after Momma Ida and her mom died within days of each other. Sherry would tag along with the young couple. Even with Sherry as a "chaperone," Momma and Dad's relationship revolved around drinking and sneaking around.

The turning point in my parents' relationship occurred when Momma got pregnant in the summer of 1962. Upon finding out about Momma's pregnancy, Bigma was furious and immediately took her to a "friend's house" to abort the baby. The horrific incident that followed was not a medical procedure but an invasive, unsterilized, and extremely painful process. They used household utensils, castor oil, and soda pop. It was used as punishment for allowing herself to get pregnant. Momma was then told to never speak of it again. More secrets. This was a moment in Momma's life that she would never forget, nor forgive. She was also told never to see Henry again. I can only imagine the confusion in Momma's head and heart. Momma knew that no one disobeyed Bigma, but she loved Henry because he was her protector. He never laid a hand on her and truly wanted to be with her. Cousin Sherry and Momma shared a bedroom. Momma never told Sherry what happened, yet somehow Sherry knew.

In 1965, Momma and Dad secretly eloped before she graduated high school. She told me once everyone found out, they thought she was pregnant again, but she wasn't. My dad enlisted in the Army shortly thereafter, and around 1966, was sent to Vietnam after basic training in Colorado and Hawaii where they had moved. Momma enjoyed life in

Hawaii while Dad was in Vietnam and started a little part time job while she was there. She was away from Bigma, living on her own when she became pregnant again in 1968. She didn't consume alcohol during her pregnancy, and she did everything that was recommended. She talked about really enjoying this time in her life because it gave her a sense of freedom she'd never experienced before.

When news came of Dad's pending discharge, Momma was getting close to delivering, so he decided to send Momma home. She didn't want to return, she wanted to stay in Hawaii. She was supposed to go live with his parents, but Bigma wouldn't allow it. She later told me, she really wished she had gone to live with his mother, Grandma Ruby, instead.

Bigma saved up enough money and in 1969 she bought her own home, a two-family flat. It was a brick home, with four bedrooms, a full basement, and a two-car garage. There were three vacant lots attached and Bigma used these as her garden. This was a definite step up from the life Bigma came from in Louisiana. It was known as the "big house on the corner." The neighborhood was close with each house filled with families and children. There were quite a few grandparent-led households such as ours. Momma had gone to school with a lot of our neighbors, so everyone knew everyone.

My mom and her older sister Vera were both pregnant at the time when Bigma bought her house. Aunt Vera's husband and oldest child were tragically killed in a car accident. Both of Bigma's daughters lived with her while awaiting the birth of their babies. The babies were born eight days apart.

I was a healthy baby girl, born on February 15, 1969, and Dad returned shortly thereafter. Bigma didn't care for my dad Henry, so he wasn't always welcomed into her home when he came to visit me. The three of us lived together for a short time because I can remember living in an upper flat in a different neighborhood. So, I believe they tried to make their marriage work, but it didn't last too long and soon Momma and I were living with Bigma again.

Momma said it was Bigma's meddling and the dislike between the two families that caused them to split. Bigma was a controller and felt everyone should do what she said. I'm sure Dad wasn't having any parts of that, but Momma didn't know how to say "no" to her mother. There wasn't any support from Bigma to encourage their young marriage to work.

In 1971, there was some gossip about Dad and Momma's best friend. Dad was supposed to have been the father of the best friend's son. Needless to say, this put a further strain on their relationship. Momma and Dad divorced in 1974, the year after Momma delivered my brother Kenneth. My dad was not Kenneth's father.

Momma and Dad as teenagers.

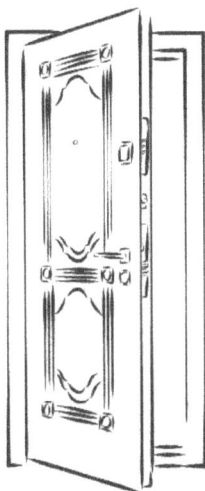

FOUR

Momma began working. She would take public transportation to drop us off at the babysitters then go to work only to reverse the process in the evening. If Bigma babysat, which she often did, she expected to get paid. Bigma didn't play when it came to her coins even when she was caring for her grandchildren.

Even though I was young, (probably around four or five years old), my heart was stirred to try to protect Momma in these dark times. My memories flood back to me still …

My eyes opened to the soft sounds of Marvin Gaye singing, "What's Going On?" I made my way out of the bed, climbing over the wooden slats of a crib, to the floor and towards the door. As I slowly opened it, the music grew much louder. I walked down the short hallway with its light blue painted walls that led into the dining room. There was a table and four chairs. Momma was sitting at the table; her head was down, and the room was dark. The curtains were pulled shut but there were drips of sunlight seeping through the worn cracks of the curtain material and around the window frame. On the table was a bottle which was all too familiar. A brown bottle of E and J Brandy.

I walked towards Momma who hadn't raised her head yet and I touched her face. Her skin was so soft and oh ...wet. She's been crying again. As she lifted her head, she smiled and reached to pick me up. She was so little, a mere 100 pounds dripping wet, but she managed to pick me up so I could sit on her lap. She wrapped me up tightly in her arms and hummed the Marvin Gaye lyrics. The record player in the living room spilled out the sounds of trumpets and piano to the tune again and she began to sing boldly. The lyrics strangely matched an unspoken grief in her heart. Then she told me to go get some clothes and get ready. I obediently turned and walked back down the pale blue hallway when I heard her. She was crying again, this time hard, long sobs. She lifted the glass to take another sip. *Hopefully, this sip will take away the pain*, I was sure she was thinking. I ran back to her and tightly hugged her small body in the torn silver and pink nightgown. *I can protect you,* I say within myself. *I can protect you.* Tears spring from my eyes as I listened to her sniffles as she attempted to stop herself from crying. It didn't work.

This would be the first memory of many where I tried to protect Momma from the demons, memories, and dark episodes of her life. The reality was that I needed protection from my own demons, memories, and dark episodes. Too many to count.

That's when I found my bedroom closet, my safe place.

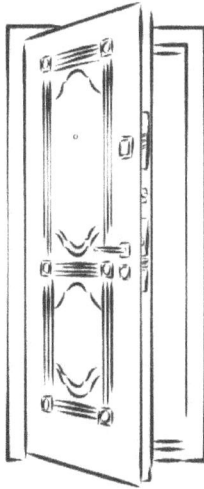

FIVE

Momma, my brother Kenny and I all lived in the upper part of Bigma's two family flat on Grand and 12th street. It was located less than a mile from where the 1967 Detroit riots happened. The ruins of businesses and homes were still evident and almost signaled a sense of history many would've like to have forgotten. As a single mother with two kids, Momma depended on Bigma to watch after us when she worked or when we were left home alone—which was often. I always had this underlying drive to protect my brother which wasn't easy; he was a wild one! There is only a four-year age gap between us, but I always knew it was my responsibility (that word was drilled into me) to take care of him.

Our flat had two-bedrooms, a living room, dining room, kitchen, and back porch which was above Bigma's family room. In the dining room, there was a standalone bar, and a table and chair set. The living room was furnished with a couch, coffee table, floor model record player and a TV on a stand. Momma was very proud of how she worked to furnish her place, while taking care of her kids as a single mom.

Momma struggled with low self-esteem and relationship insecurities. She wanted to be in a solid relationship at any cost, including her dignity. Momma always worked to provide for me and Kenneth but also to buy liquor to feed her habit. It was a vicious, dysfunctional life but I can say she did the best she could while dealing with her addiction.

There were several live-in boyfriends that would come and go in Momma's life. She genuinely loved them all and I believed some of them cared about her, but their actions were completely opposite. The most dangerous was her first boyfriend after my dad. I cannot forget his name or his face. Harvey was very abusive towards my mom especially when they drank, which was every day. He was very tall, with a milk chocolate complexion. He kept his hair in a low-cut afro which extended into his mustache and beard. He was a very handsome man. Their relationship was volatile to say the least and it didn't matter who was around.

During their relationship, I witnessed the most violent fights and sexual encounters between the two of them. When the memories come, I often wonder if this was consensual or forced upon her. All of which ended with Momma's face and body covered with bruises and sometimes broken bones. Alcohol was always her go to, it would numb the pain she felt emotionally, mentally, and physically. You would think that Bigma would've intervened, but I cannot recall one time that she did, until the end. Bigma helped Momma to put a plan in motion in order to get Harvey out of the house and out of her life.

One night, my brother and I were told to sleep downstairs in Bigma's extra room. As we walked through the kitchen entering the flat, I remember seeing a pot of water boiling on the stove. This pot was usually used to hold the delectable soups she often made in the winter months. We were told, "no matter what you hear, do not come out of the bedroom." I laid in the twin size bed, wrapped in warm fluffy blankets with the scent of wax candles.

My momma's bedroom was right above us, so I heard it all. Momma and Harvey were yelling back and forth in a heated argument which wasn't much of a surprise. Then there was silence. Bigma's kitchen door creaked open which meant she was going up stairs. Then a short time later, I heard Harvey yell extremely loud and then the thump of someone falling out of the bed. There were more screams, yelling, and loud thumps on the floor. The story was later told that Momma and Bigma threw boiling, hot water on Harvey's naked body. He left that night, never to return to the house again.

Momma loved Bigma and wanted love from her and at the same time Momma wanted to be free of the life that came with being Bigma's youngest daughter. Momma's life was continuous cycles of domestic violence, sexual abuse (some at the coaching of Bigma), and alcoholism. Momma tried numerous times to stop drinking and smoking cigarettes only to fall back into the same pattern. My brother Kenneth grew up not really knowing who his father was, there was always some speculation; especially since he carries two different men's names. His middle name is related to Harvey's full name and another part is from my dad. He believes Harvey is his father. He said he was told this by Momma when he became an adult.

There were nights when the fights between Momma and her boyfriends would go into the morning hours, and she had to call off from work and I would be late for school. She couldn't go into work with the bruises, lack of sleep, and a hangover. Momma would keep the curtains closed, while sitting at the dining room table …. drinking and listening to the blues on that old record player. I know now she was suffering from depression. There were days she wouldn't come out of her bedroom … just drinking and sleeping. It was how she coped.

While all of this was going on, no one ever talked about what happened in our home. We all abided by the previously mentioned motto of "what happens at the house stays at the house," and we never spoke of it.

All these years later, I physically react to having been a child closed up in her world. A dark house triggers memories of a darkness I could not escape. When I need to feel safe, I go to my closet or find a similar space. I desperately wanted to protect her from the pain …each time hoping that this would be the last she would suffer. I longed for Momma to be happy.

I can't remember the circumstances, but we moved out of my grandmother's upper flat into the basement of a home belonging to a friend of one of Momma's boyfriends. Leo and Kim were a mixed couple, he was Black, and she was Vietnamese. They met when Leo served in the Army during the Vietnam war. They married and he brought her back to the States with him when he was discharged. I can remember some of these Army buddies' conversations. They were good friends, yet I don't remember Leo ever mistreating Kim the way Momma was mistreated. In fact, it was the opposite. I can see Kim's beautifully round olive-skinned face as she would yell at Leo speaking Vietnamese so we couldn't figure out what they were talking about. I don't remember how long we lived with them, but I do remember the tension between Kim and Momma. It was Kim's house, but my mom had two children that lived in the basement of their home. Kim was always loving towards me as I can recall but that time living with them wasn't pleasant.

One night, as my mom and her boyfriend were sleeping, my brother Kenny began to cry. I believe he was around two or three months old. He was hungry but they didn't move, so I got up and tried to stop him from crying. He wore cloth diapers and was very wet. I'd watched as his diaper was changed so I knew how it was done. I removed the rubber pants, unpinned the soiled diaper and put a new diaper on him, making sure to pin the diaper tight but he continued to cry. They never moved, nor did they get up to see what was wrong. He cried and cried. I tried to comfort him, but nothing helped. Finally, Kim came downstairs to see what was wrong. She took Kenny from me and realized I had pinned the diaper to his skin. Kim took care of the baby while I sat there crying. I didn't mean to hurt the baby. Deep pain still sinks down into my heart. This is one of the few memories that still brings me to tears. I didn't take care of the baby … he was my responsibility.

Kim woke my mom and in a very harsh tone filled with a mixture of English and Vietnamese curse words, she told my mom to get up and take care of her baby. Soon after, we moved back in with Bigma.

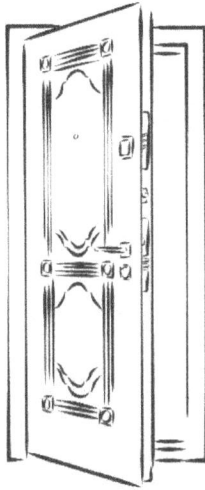

SIX

Bigma believed in hustling to make sure she could take care of herself and her family. Her gambling parties could turn into sex parties if the price was right. She would do just about anything that people were willing to try. She also rented her second room to a Louisiana drifter named Lionel, but we all affectionately called him Horsey. I have so many fond memories of Horsey taking care of the household repairs, cooking, yard work, and gardening while taking care of us kids. He was definitely a Louisiana outdoorsman, and he shared many interesting and colorful stories of his life in the south as a Black man.

Horsey and Bigma lived together for as long as I can remember until he died of cancer in 1987. I loved Horsey so much because he took care of her home and took care of us. When I say us, I mean my brother, myself, and my first cousins from Aunt Vera and Uncle Matt. So, while Bigma hosted the parties, fed the participants, and kept the liquor flowing, my mom was responsible for collecting the money and handling the business end of things. Horsey was the muscle, but would turn into part of the entertainment after a few bottles of liquor. It's no wonder cancer took his life because he would wake up with a glass of gin every morning and end the day having drank several bottles of his favorite liquors. The shadows in his eyes would soften after the first drink.

Horsey often had conversations with ghosts. His Louisiana accent would thicken like molasses, and we knew his visitor wasn't from this world. It was part of the culture. He would tell us colorful stories of spirits walking in the plantation fields. As kids, we would sit around the family room, eager to hear of the spirits that chased him through the middle of the night in the cotton fields of Louisiana.

"I was walking through the fields, and I couldn't see my hand in front of my face," he would say. We would ask how he knew the way to get home. He would tell us that people had a keen sense of direction and just learned how to follow the paths or the rows through the fields. He would also explain how you could recognize the trees and where the moon was positioned. But one night he was walking alone and heard footsteps behind him, matching his, stride for stride.

"I turned around but didn't see anything. I walked faster and so did the footsteps! At this point, I broke out into a full run and the footsteps chased me close behind. When I made it close enough to the one bedroom shack me, Momma, and Leroy (his brother) lived in, I ran around the shack several times yelling for someone to open the door. By the third go round, Leroy opened the door laughing and I ran inside!" This is the sound of Louisiana, the sound of ghost walking and Black folks laughing. We had no idea if this colorful story of ghosts was true, but it was enough for us kids. It was better than any bedtime story. It was better than what was happening in our house.

Horsey was a hard-working man and would do anything for Bigma. But that was not always enough for her, she needed to be in control. If Horsey tried to take the lead on anything or stand up against her, she would become angry. Just like everyone else, he paid the price. They fought constantly. I remember a time when Bigma became so outraged in her drunken state, she went into her back room, got her small pistol and shot him in the side. He refused to let it be known that she was the one that shot him. He cleaned himself up, had my mom drive him to the hospital and said that someone shot him while he was walking home. All the while my cousins and I were in the family room, listening to music when the fight broke out, and the gun came out. We adored Horsey, so this was devastating, but not uncommon to see. All the while Bigma was blaming it on him because he went against what she wanted. The crazy part is Horsey said she was right.

Even though Bigma and Horsey never married they lived as husband and wife. They enjoyed traveling and would take us kids on family trips. Because they both were from the South, they would travel back to Louisiana every winter in the family mobile home. They would also go back South because Bigma had extremely bad arthritis and the cold northern air would make her body creak and groan. It took the South to soothe her out again. It was one of many ways Horsey would care for Bigma. While they were in the South, they would do a lot of hunting and fishing which was one of the things that we looked forward to as kids. They always brought back a huge crate of live seafood filled with crab, shrimps, lobster, and crawfish. We couldn't wait until they got back because it meant a seafood feast like no other!

Horsey and his friends would go to Metro Airport to retrieve the crate and Bigma would prepare the big pot of boiling water. She always kept a cabinet full of seasonings and spices from the South which she would pull out to mix in the huge pot. Bigma kept modern appliances and a newly renovated kitchen because she loved to cook huge family meals. It was nothing for me to come home from school to find live chickens, turkeys, rabbits, frogs, or turtles roaming around in the backyard that later would wind up as our dinner. Bigma was famous for her parties, meals, and a quick temper but no one ever left her house hungry!

Once the crate of seafood arrived, we would watch in amazement as Bigma would grab the critters out of the crate and throw them into the pot of boiling water. We would cover the table in the family room and the sunroom with newspaper, grab the nutcrackers, melted butter and seasonings, and wait patiently for the seafood to be dumped on the table. I can still smell the Cajun spices and see the steam rising from the table of food. My older cousin and I would crack open the crab shells for the meat while sucking the Cajun juice out of the legs. Our little brothers struggled a bit, so we would crack open the shells for them and leave them on the table so they had the fun of pulling out jewels of buttered meat. I can still taste the crawfish today.

Bigma and Horsey's garden was one that was envied in the neighborhood; filled with rows and rows of vegetables. Bigma planted corn, squash, okra, tomatoes, collard greens, turnips, mustard greens and let's not forget those darn green beans which we had to shell and bag at the end of the summer! The grandchildren helped work the garden to prepare for planting. Every Saturday we were given tasks and chores around the house which included the garden. We learned how to till the garden in preparation for the seeding. Then there was the daily, or even weekly upkeep of turning the dirt and watering the garden. Horsey was known for sitting in the yard with a rifle to ward off rodents that would get to the vegetables. I can still smell the fresh dirt fertilizer mix intertwined in my fingers, under my nails, down in my ears, and up my nose. It was those times that I felt the most at peace.

I can still hear the music playing from Bigma's cabinet stereo blaring Motown music favorites. Marvin Gaye, The Temptations, The O'Jays and such blues greats as BB King. There often some of the raunchiest music you could have heard during that time. It wasn't uncommon to wake up to the music, knowing it was time to get to work. We were rewarded greatly because Bigma loved to cook. That was her love language. It was during these times where her actions were inconsistent with the pain she inflicted on her family.

I watched the excitement of people coming and going, enjoying the flow of food, drinks, and sex. There were gambling tables, music, dancing for hours and hustlers setting up their next score. Into the night there were the effects of drunken sleepovers, party trash, dirty dishes, throughout the house and Momma's alcoholic spirals. Then came the cleanup from the drunken fights over a card game or someone's girlfriend. I watched with excitement and with much wonder. This was normal. But there were many times the fights and arguments erupted so quickly that I may not have had time to retreat to my closet for safety. I learned how to try and defuse the situation or freeze in the moment.

These times occurred especially when Momma and Bigma would get into heated arguments or physical fights. Watching this as a young child, I was taught by Momma to never put my hands on her. She instilled in me a fear so deep that she could literally hurt me. I knew it was possible because she had to fight to defend herself. I feared my mother, just as she feared her own mother. I learned from her how to duck when a hand was raised against me just like she ducked so well from her own mother. My body learned to react when it felt someone walking behind me.

Momma said she first started drinking when she was really young because Bigma loaned her out to one of her male friends. It was her way to escape the abuse and constant manipulation of Bigma. Bigma knew the art of bullying, but she couldn't be bullied. If you refused to listen to her, Bigma would cut you out of her life and swear up and down it was because of what you did. She was never wrong; it was always the actions of others. Whenever Bigma would get angry with Momma, she would lock her kitchen door. Because we lived in a two-family flat, both flats were accessible by a set of stairs which led into the kitchens of each unit. Bigma never locked her kitchen door and neither did we. So once into the lower level of the home, anyone could access either unit through the kitchen doors. That was the primary way we would enter Bigma's unit. If she was angry with us, specifically Momma, she would lock the kitchen door and not speak to either of us until Momma would concede to Bigma's wishes. This could go on for weeks! As a child, this hurt deeply because I enjoyed spending time with Bigma. As mean as she was, she was my grandmother and I loved being with her. I didn't know life any other way, besides she was a great cook! So many of our meals were from her kitchen.

In every sense of the word Bigma was the matriarch of our family, there would never be anyone like her ever again. She left a legacy of strength and endurance. She is a cornerstone in our family history. She fought hard for her family, for her life, and her beliefs. Carrie was not afraid to go against anything that threatened her life. Oh, how I often wished I possessed her strength and her deep-seated need to fight. Looking back over Bigma's life, I see a woman that had limited options and defied great odds that were against her. No, she wasn't perfect, and she made choices that affected generations to follow but she did what she thought was best to survive. She was a survivor of horrific odds. Born into a family two generations short of slavery and living in the deep south, in the backwoods of Louisiana, she learned how to survive with limited education afforded to a colored person only to be used to provide for her family and herself. She became a mother and wife at the age of sixteen and I honestly don't know if she had any future plans for herself. She did the best that she could based on what she knew and what she was exposed to. Up until this point I resented her greatly because of what I experienced as a young girl at her hands. But I can only imagine the life she had with the unlimited amount of trauma she endured. She only did what she thought was right for herself and her family. I remember sharing a sexual assault with her that I had experienced, her response was "you need to get over it, it happened long ago." There was no compassion in her voice, or a reassuring hug from Bigma that everything would be okay. I believe now that was her way of teaching me to deal with it, by just getting over it.

We have words now to describe what she experienced. She fought to survive and was often triggered by her experiences and the actions of others. When triggered, she immediately reverted into fight mode. When challenged she took on an alpha approach to stand her ground. When needed, she utilized whatever resources necessary to provide for herself and her children, even if it meant using her children. It wasn't uncommon for sex to be used as a method of survival. Her love language was providing and feeding everyone that was hungry. She didn't hug or kiss her family a lot, it was a sign of weakness and she needed strength to survive. Yet when she loved, she loved with her full heart. I remember times as a child, when I would go and lay my head on her lap that was formed by those big pretty legs. She would run her fingers through my hair until I fell asleep. I can still smell the Oil of Olay lotion she wore; it was her distinct scent. It wasn't too strong but a faint smell that reminded me of the smell of fresh air. I loved the smell of air and fresh dirt especially when digging for worms that we would often take on fishing trips. It was those memories that I had to fight to recall through all the hurt that I experienced.

Now, years later, as a grandmother, myself, I cherish those moments I had with Bigma. It drives me to shower my grandson Matthew with hugs and kisses. He loves to hold hands while sitting in my lap. I pray he will remember those moments just like I remember those moments with Bigma.

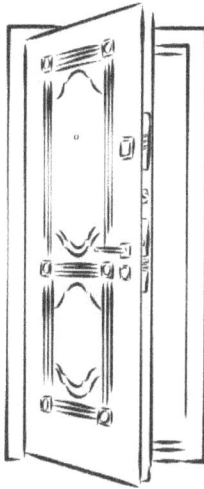

SEVEN

Living with Bigma and Momma I watched these women push through their own demons, struggles and trauma to achieve great strides from where they started. Every parent wants more for their child and I can see that being the root of a lot of their indiscretions.

It was difficult to live in our house because Bigma was in complete control. She ruled the family, and she definitely ruled her house. There were many days when she would turn the heat off because she could. The thermostat was on her floor, so we learned how to layer up, bundle up and wait for her to get out of her mood. My mom paid rent, bills and raised me and my brother. She did the best that she could, but being an alcoholic, the liquor always came for her. There were days or nights when she wouldn't come home because she was somewhere drunk or she would leave home sober but somehow managed to stop along the way before getting home at 4:30 p.m., stumbling into the house. She had tried to quit on her own, but shadows of the demons crossed her face until she took another drink.

Internally, my emotions were all over the place while my mother was drunk. I even told her so when I was much older, all she could say was "I'm sorry I didn't know." And I honestly believe her because she would black out for a day or two and wouldn't remember anything that happened. In those times, I learned to take care of her and protect my brother as best as I could as a child, and then as a teenager. I learned to take care of not only my mom, but whatever was going on in the house. I became a fixer, but I would also flee if I couldn't head off the battles that were going on. I would run to my closet.

My closet was my safe place. I would often drag my brother in there too. We received Bible tracts from the church ladies who came to our elementary school on Wednesdays for an afterschool program. I would hide the tracts in the closet so I could read the prayers while we were in there waiting out the storm. I remember praying to God … *Destroy them. Kill and beat down all the people that hurt me.* I knew I was not only referencing those strangers that were in my house, but also my mom because of the pain that I was dealing with and everything we had to endure. Those were my child-like prayers. But God never came; He never sent the angel to wipe them out, there was always tomorrow. And tomorrow would come and we would start all over again.

I began experiencing depression as early as the age of eight or nine. It could've been before then. It was easier to go with the flow in order to survive the parties, the fights, and the drunken weekends. The touches, the smell of alcohol, old musty body odors, and the faces. The rough, scraggly, brittle beards against my face, then the fight within myself to survive through the violation of my body. Momma couldn't protect me; she didn't know how. There were those secrets I couldn't speak of or were told to forget about. They would creep up in my dreams.

It was easier to stay awake so I would not have to deal with them or so that I would know when someone was coming through my door. I developed a sixth sense for when something was going down. That feeling in the pit of my stomach was a good indicator, so I began to trust my gut, talking to myself and trying to calm the storm brewing within me. I could read facial expressions or body language well and knew what to do to ease the tension or get Kenny and myself out of the way. If we could make it to the closet, then they wouldn't find us. That small little closet smelled of oak wood, musty clothes, and old shoes with the two-tone colors of a pale blue and off white on the walls and ceiling. Some of Momma's clothes hung in there because she shared her closet with whichever boyfriend was living with us at the time.

My bedroom was large enough for two twin-sized beds, and a dresser, which, at the time, I shared with my brother. There were two windows, one overlooking the back of the house, closest to the two-car garage and the other gave me a good view of our neighbors houses since we were the corner house. I remember sitting in my bedroom, often looking out of the window, and wishing I could live anywhere else to escape the hell that was happening in our home.

Momma continued to go through many abusive relationships which were all fueled by alcohol and sex. The enemy used whatever could numb them to manipulate and to control two generations of women in my family. There wasn't a man that could handle the power and strength the women in my family possessed. That strength was necessary for survival. But it came at a tremendous cost for the next generation.

I learned to put on an emotional front when taking care of Momma. I would sometimes find her passed out drunk, beaten up from another fight with one of "them" or a bad argument with her mother. I would put on a strong front, only later to break down in sobs of tears because I had to bottle it up inside. My thought process was, *first, take care of her or them.* But who was there for me to talk to or to look for to protect me from them or from her? Why did she hit me when I crawled into myself? So, I learned to embrace the darkness that was calling my name. I learned over time to keep my feelings to myself, but my emotions would come out in my tears. Momma would yell at me to stop crying … "Why are you crying! Stop being so weak! What are you crying for? You're always crying!" Oh God, how many times did I hear that in my life! The emotions would be so great that the tears would just start coming and I couldn't turn them off until I could convince myself the threat was over or was able to retreat to my closet. I cried whether I was happy, sad, scared … I just cried.

The tears hid my true feelings and my true self. I felt that if people knew who I really was, they wouldn't like me. They would reject me, wouldn't like what they saw, and hurt me again. I don't know which one was worse, but I knew Katrina couldn't seep through, she had to stay hidden, protected.

Katrina wasn't valued enough to be loved unconditionally. She didn't deserve it. Her worth was tied to her family, environment, and upbringing. She could only get what was left because beautiful people got first pick. In order for people to accept her, she had to please. She had to learn what they liked then made sure to deliver every time. What are friends? Who are friends? How does she make friends? She pleases … but then to make real friends, she had to keep making up a story of who she was. If they knew the real her, the friendship wouldn't last long.

That was the dialog that ran continuously through my soul. The trauma I experienced as a child defined who I was or so I thought. I believed the lies of the enemy that said I had to compromise my soul in order to be liked. Yet the harder I tried, the deeper I slipped into a darkness within myself.

Then there was the inconsistent presence of my father. He was dealing with his own demons. I began to look for that love, protection, and security from everyone else. I first had to learn to be the protector of Momma and my Kenny. She needed protection. He needed protection. There was no time for tears because tears showed weakness. But the tears came out of fear which I couldn't hide. I was either not strong enough or working hard enough to protect because I showed my weakness through my tears. I hid the emptiness Katrina felt and "Trina" depended on it.

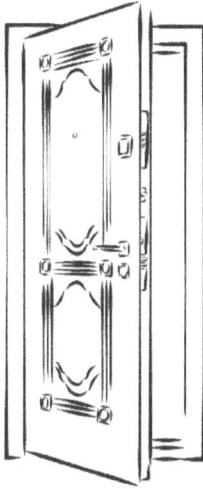

EIGHT

I was around nine years old, when we started attending church. It was actually Momma's Dad's church, just a few miles from our house. Even though Granddad was still married to the same woman, (not Bigma), he began to rebuild his relationship with his adult children. Granddad was stoic in his deliveries of the Gospel and set in his ways but truly loved the Lord and could *preach and sang*! He preached with power and conviction. Momma and Granddad's relationship progressed over the years, which was something they both always wanted. He wanted a relationship with his children but also carried a guilt about not being there for them when they were growing up. He said he tried, but Bigma wasn't the easiest person to get along with and his (crazy in the head as he would call her), wife didn't make it easy either. His wife was a heavy drinker also, which led to her being very abusive to her husband and children. I think had he wanted to, he could have stood up against the women in his life who appeared to dominate his world. After all, he preached and taught how the Bible confirms the man is the leader and the head of his household. Yet he never stood up in that capacity.

He was dedicated to the church he was called to pastor, this little storefront church, New Missionary Baptist Church. We began attending the church when Momma was in her early thirties. As a matter of fact, everyone in our community attended church, it was a part of our upbringing. Wednesday night Bible study and Saturday afternoon choir rehearsal were common. Sundays were set aside for church and the activities around it: Sunday school, church service, dinner at church and then afternoon service. Nothing got done on Sundays except church. Granddad really loved having his family participate *in something he loved*. He loved the Lord, and he loved preaching. His sister and her family of nine children attended along with many other large families. It's what Black folks did.

Along with worshiping, praising, foot stomping, singing, and preaching, lurking in the background was alcohol, adultery, domestic abuse, and stealing; all of which Granddad tried to keep a handle on. He had a weakness towards aggressive women … it was something he couldn't fight against. Now that I look back, those were the women he was drawn to. But when it came to his kids, within boundaries, he did everything he could for them and then he focused on his grandchildren. His grandchildren were the apples of his eye, but everything revolved around the church. His priorities were in this order: church, God, family, and church.

In the eighties, he grew in the Lord and in the ministry. Granddad took each fight with his wife silently and tried to focus on running a church, being present in his family's life, and being a husband and stepfather. Whenever his kids or grandkids needed him, he was there, but nothing came before that church.

As his relationship with Momma grew, so did his dependence on her. They became very close, and I believe he was the reason she went into recovery for drinking in 1986. Granddad knew of her lifestyle with the men and the drinking, but I'm not sure if he knew about the sexual abuse she endured.

I still remember the day she decided to go into recovery. She walked into the living room where me and my brother were watching TV to announce she was leaving for a month and going to a hospital in Chelsea, Michigan, for in-patient therapy. It was what she needed to get her life together. There were so many emotions around her getting clean from everyone, especially Granddad. He supported her decision and her journey every step of the way. Bigma told her, "You should've done this a long time ago." Yet she never discouraged the continued crazy behavior.

While Momma was at the rehab hospital, she had a plan for her family and friends to take care of us while she was gone. The people she depended on really didn't want the responsibility of caring for us in her absence. Only her friend Carol did, and she kept her word when everyone else was done after the first week. Momma called and asked Carol to bring my brother, myself, and Bigma for a family session. At first, Bigma said she wasn't going to come, but "Harry" the counselor, explained the importance of everyone who Momma felt was significant in her life needing to attend. Bigma came. Bigma hesitantly joined the group as we sat in a warm cozy, log cabin styled room. The room had comfy sofas, a fireplace with a roaring hot fire that illuminated the small room, and a coffee table with lots of snacks for me and my brother (we were fourteen and seventeen). Carol was asked to sit in another room as this was a family session. My brother sat closest to Momma while I sat on the other end of the sofa and Bigma sat across from all of us clutching her purse. With a defiant look on her face, Bigma was clearly uncomfortable and did not want to be there. Harry was a thin build, White man with a brownish colored mustache and beard. What I remember most about Harry was the sound of his voice. His voice was so calm as he began to explain that the session was the opportunity for Momma to share what she felt was necessary in her process of recovery with the family.

Momma began by telling us how much she loved us and was so glad she took these steps to get back on the right track. Then she turned to me and my brother, "I'm so sorry I put you all through so much while I was drinking. I haven't been a good mother to you because the majority of the time I was passed out drunk or too drunk to even remember what I did. I needed to get away to take care of myself so I can do a better job of being a mother. I'm sorry for everything I've done, and I hope you accept my apology."

My brother looked at my face to see what I was going to say. He knew I was very angry with Momma for leaving us to go to rehab now that I was no longer a child. I couldn't take it anymore. I knew it was necessary for her to recover, especially because of the environment we lived in, but why couldn't she have done this sooner? Why put us through all the torment and trauma she faced only now to say it was the alcohol and "I'm sorry?" Where were you when he touched me? How could you allow him to abuse me? Just last week you didn't acknowledge my presence for over a week because I asked for your attention and love, the same attention that you would give to my younger brother. I was a child trying to handle adult issues, but you saw it as my responsibility to take care of you when you were drunk and make sure my brother was provided for. Sorry, it wasn't good enough, especially when I had to cover the bills and step in as mama while you were gone for thirty days. And now, it's all better because you said, "I'm sorry?"

I was so angry, but I did as I always would and said I forgave her and was happy she was sober. The emotional weight of everything we had experienced in the early years of my childhood was so draining on me at this point. Just like many other times, I put my emotions to the side, put on that "it's alright" face and kept it moving. I had learned by this time to stop expecting emotional support from those closest to me because they didn't have it to give. Through all of the fights, arguments, beatings, and sexual abuse in our home, only for me to act as if it was normal … this was it for me with her. I had had enough. In my head, I thought to myself, *how long will this last? A week, a month, we will see.* To be absolutely honest, I didn't believe her at all.

Then Momma turned to Bigma to apologize. She began to talk about the issues that had plagued her life, beginning with Bigma's attempted abortion of her and the sexual abuse. Bigma became very defensive and said she wouldn't take the blame for Momma's drinking. As Bigma angrily said it wasn't her fault with a snarl, I saw Momma shrink back like a child. Tears ran down her face as she apologized again to Bigma who definitely wouldn't communicate with her or Harry who tried to defuse the hostility in the room. Harry got a piece of Bigma's mind too as she got up from the couch and headed to the door yelling for Carol to take her home. My brother and I hugged Momma and told her it would be okay, and hurriedly left the room before we were left behind. As we walked out of the room, I could hear Harry say, "I see what you're talking about, yet you can do this without her help."

Fortunately, that major blow up didn't deter Momma from her track of sobriety, she was determined to do it this time and she did. She would often say, "As I started to go through the detoxing symptoms, I prayed and asked God to deliver me from this. He did and immediately I lost the taste for alcohol. I never took another drink or thought about it after that." In hindsight, I am so proud of my mom. She overcame some difficult situations as a child but still found the strength to take on the fight of her life … for her life.

In place of alcohol, she found a new outlet for herself and began crocheting blankets. She shared this creative gift with many family members and friends and passed it onto me. To this day, I crochet baby blankets as gifts for newborns in our family and among our friends.

Granddad would often tell Momma to "take care of your mom, no matter what, take care of your mom." She took that to heart, because despite everything Bigma did to Momma, she never stopped trying to please her. I recently considered this parallel between myself and my momma. Granddad encouraged Momma to "trust in the Lord" and become more active in the church, which she did. After going to rehab, she became completely devoted to the Lord and to the church. She was elected church secretary in the early nineties, a position she held until his passing. Being a part of the pastor's family wasn't easy because he endured a lot from the members and we pretty much watched from the sidelines. He would say, "The devil is after this church and after me." Yet Momma stuck by her daddy's side through it all. Having her father actively in her life even though their relationship didn't really start until she was an adult, pulled her off the self-destructive path I strongly believe she would have continued down. Granddad began coming by the house to check on us, including Bigma. He slowly transitioned into the role of father and grandfather. He became my father figure.

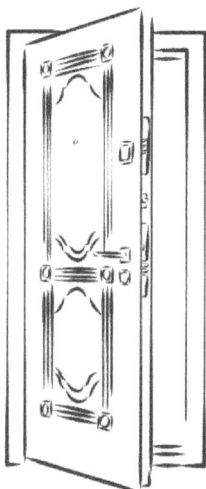

NINE

There were days I was so angry with my father until I wished him gone, then there were the times I just wanted his love. Henry McIntosh was six foot two inches, chocolate brown, lean, and strong enough to pick me up with one arm so I could hug his neck. The feel of his beard was soft and tamed as he would playfully rub it against my cheek. When in his arms, I could feel him shaking as if he was nervous, but I loved to snuggle in his embrace, shake and all. As a child, I wanted Momma and Dad to be together; he was big and strong enough to protect us. But he never knew and didn't want to know. The calvary didn't come.

Dad dealt with flashbacks and PTSD from the Vietnam war. He used to talk about the war but only in passing. Sex, drugs, and women was how he coped with it all and he had commitment issues. How could he commit to someone when he had these visions and voices running through his head? He fought in the war, but the war won. The war was nasty. He came back broken and underappreciated for his sacrifice. I can't give my dad a pass for not protecting me as a child because he could've fought for our family. As hard as he fought in the war, he could have fought just as hard for his wife and child.

The softness of women and the solitude of the drugs and alcohol would take away the emptiness and pain he felt inside but then that would fade away. How could he love what he didn't understand? Me. If only his mind could focus long enough to learn how to nurture and love me. He just wouldn't give his little girl the love and protection she longed for because it would open his eyes to what was going on. He did what came naturally, he hid from it. He would hide for days, or weeks from those that loved him. He would hide alongside someone else who didn't know what he was struggling with. Their affection didn't come with conditions or requirements. But I came with responsibility. I wanted his protection and love. He didn't know what being a father meant to Katrina or how to save me from the hell I was going through. So, he stayed away until he absolutely had to come. That's how it seemed to me as a child growing up without her father being active in her life.

Did he know what I was going through? The hungry nights, holes in my clothes and shoes, eating cereal with bugs? Did he know how bad Mama was beaten by every Tom, Dick, or Harry? Did he even care? Did he know there were nights she didn't come home, and I was up all night waiting on her? Did he know who was touching me, abusing me? Did he know how bad she beat me?

He didn't want to know. He was dealing with his own demons. He wore a mask, just like my Momma. Just like me.

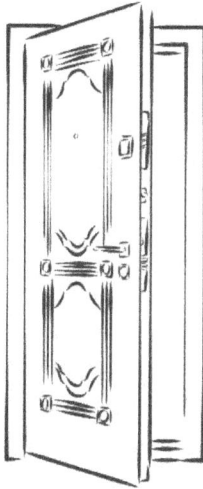

TEN

In my teenage years, I was very promiscuous and free with my body. I did not and would not set boundaries. Sex and alcohol were my drugs of choice. There were nights when I would sneak out so that I could be with someone, anyone, who I felt could meet the emotional needs that I had. But they were only temporary and sometimes painful. Emotionally, "Trina" had to figure out how to keep Katrina safe yet strive to meet the emotional need that I longed for.

I had been pregnant several times by then and chose to end each pregnancy. There was no way I could take care of a child and take care of myself.

Besides, if Momma found out, I could only imagine the actions that would occur. Momma tried everything that she could to keep me from going down the wrong path. It was what I saw all my life, it was all I knew, and it helped to bury the pain that I was feeling. She would get so angry with me, but I just could not bring myself to tell her she was my example. Momma yelled and screamed at me to not make the same mistakes that she did. I thought it was hypocritical of her to be so angry with me about what I was doing when she couldn't remember that I saw her and was often in the room when the same thing happened. She couldn't remember, but I did. The brain remembers every traumatic experience that the body has gone through. When those memories are triggered, the body will respond accordingly to protect itself. Most of the time it is an unconscious reaction.

Looking back to my teenage years, I realize that I was triggered often, and my response was that I needed and wanted to feel safe. That primal desire usually fueled me to act in the way most familiar to me in order to get that need fulfilled. The closet was still there, and even in my teenage years I would retreat to it just to have that safe place. But emotionally the hurt and the pain never went away.

The enemy would've had me thinking I was doomed by God. My tears hid my hurt well, or so I thought. The alcohol and drugs only covered it up for a little while. Always temporary. I prayed to God, asking Him to deliver me from the hell that was brewing in my body ... but I felt that the prayers went unanswered. I had no idea what God was up to.

My years now have been full of hindsight. The mistakes, the challenges, the ups and downs, the lessons, consequences, hurdles, accomplishments, hope, conditions, setbacks, and fulfillments—I think I've experienced all of these and then some.

One important evening, I was out hanging with some friends at the end of the boulevard near the Detroit River. It was a beautiful summer night, and the parking lot was full of everyone old enough to hang out in the wee hours of the morning. There was a full moon, and the sky was full of stars twinkling to the beat of the music. We were partying, drinking, smoking, and passing the time. It was late but no one cared. I just had to make it to church before 11:00 a.m. the next day. I was good.

I needed to go to the restroom, and I asked another female to walk with me. The restroom was across the parking lot closest to the river. I remember we started walking, and then the next thing I knew, I was waking up in the field. I was completely naked, lying alone in the grass.

I didn't know what happened to me or who happened to me. All I knew was I was alone. I remember lying there listening to the music from the cars, wondering if anyone realized I was gone. Of course not, why would they? I began to cry as I lay there looking up at the stars and a full moon. I cried out, "Things have to change, LORD! I cannot continue to live my life this way. I'm heading for a road of destruction, God help me!" I made up my mind that that was it. I began to plead to the Lord, "Lord if You bring me out of this, I will never put myself in this situation again." I prayed with everything in my body, put on my clothes, and went back to the group. I can't remember if I had driven myself and just left or had to wait until my ride was ready to go. I just know, I wasn't going to continue that risky life anymore.

As I look back, I realized this was a pivotal moment in my life. The enemy had been trying to take me out at every turn. He knew if he could get me before I truly understood the call that was on my life, I would be ineffective for the Kingdom. He knew how God was going to use this moment in my life to change the trajectory of generations to come. You see, up to this point, I didn't really know Christ. I was raised in the church and felt I learned all the things that a good Baptist would know, yet I didn't really know Jesus Christ as my Savior. I could sing the song and quote the scriptures but didn't know the extent of the grace and mercy He bestowed on me. And the enemy knew it! This night was the beginning of my spiritual journey in leaving behind scared, complacent Trina and becoming Katrina.

Within a year, I was pregnant.

PART TWO

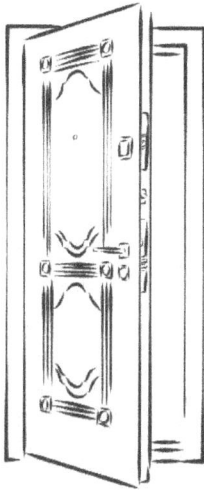

ELEVEN

The father of my baby made it clear to me, that if I pursued financial support, he wouldn't have anything to do with my baby. Later I found out, not only was he married, but he had another child! It was an emotional roller coaster trying to decide whether to continue a relationship with him for the sake of my baby or go it alone. As long as I was willing to be that warm body he could call on in the middle of the night, everything was fine. Yet, when it came time for those difficult conversations about our child or where this relationship was going, then the calls would stop. I knew being with a married man was wrong, but I wanted my child to have a father in their life, even if it meant I had to sleep with him in order for it to happen.

I knew if I kept the child, there would be a lot of criticism from the church congregation, my family, including, and especially, my mom and grandmother. My life would be completely different because of the stigma that comes with being a single parent, but I began to feel protective towards this life inside me. It was the Holy Spirit's urge for me to trust Him that made up my mind. The conversation with my mom wasn't difficult, because after all, this wasn't my first pregnancy. I was most concerned about disappointing Granddad. It was as if this was perfect timing or God's touch, but Granddad told me again, to "trust God."

As word spread through the church that the Pastor's granddaughter was having a child out of wedlock, there came the looks and comments. The older women in the church were often referred to as "Sister So-and-So" or the "Mother of the Church." One "church mother" caught me in the back of the church and began to scold me for my actions. "How could you embarrass your grandfather like this? He is the Pastor and as his granddaughter, you should've been more careful!" There was much more to this conversation pertaining to my current lifestyle, being extremely promiscuous and not following the Bible teachings. She suggested I go before the church to apologize for my actions and ask the church for forgiveness. This was common practice in the Black church when you were caught in "sin." Whenever this happened, I noticed two things, it was usually a woman, like the woman who was caught in the act of an adulterous affair. And that the men who "sinned" in the church were never brought before the congregation for a public confession.

When I told Momma what she said, she immediately told Granddad. I believe Momma had a few words for the righteous "Sister Unforgiveness" also. Granddad took a different approach and preached on the birth of Jesus. (I disclosed my pregnancy around December). "Sister Unforgiveness" must have felt the Holy Spirit's conviction after Granddad preached because that afternoon she called and asked for forgiveness. She stated, "Your grandfather preached a good sermon today about Mary's Baby. No one knew but her Who that Child would become. I kept thinking, what if she decided to turn down the assignment? We don't know who your baby will be when he grows up, he could become president!" Hence her nickname for him then became, "Mr. President."

I had been active in the church and a leader of the young children's ministry, but I was told I had to step down. In the church this was an action taken when a member openly committed a sinful act such as adultery or having a child out of wedlock. Being a member of the "first family," it was even more of a reason for this punishment.

During my pregnancy and after my baby's birth, I read my Bible. I was overwhelmed with everything I was dealing with. The pregnancy, being in a relationship with someone I didn't really like (our relationship was out of convenience because I didn't want to be alone), and slowly learning how to set boundaries but still dealing with emotional and mental issues from my childhood. It was almost too much. As I began to learn about my pregnancy and motherhood, I learned it was important to read to your baby while in the womb. So, I began to read everything I could get my hands on, and this included the entire Bible. I felt a sense of inner peace and calm in the Scriptures. Granddad told me to read the story of Hannah in 1 Samuel.

In 1 Samuel Chapter 1, Hannah was the wife of Elkanah, a Levite who was recorded as being socially prominent. Elkanah had two wives, Hannah and Peninnah. Hannah was unable to have children, but

Peninnah could. Hannah's despair was being barren in a society that valued offspring, especially male heirs. It troubled her greatly, yet Elkanah loved her despite her inability to have children.

As I began to read 1 Samuel, several things popped out at me. First, Hannah prayed for the ability to have a child, and she trusted God for this miracle. Second, when she prayed, she vowed to give the child back to God and she kept her word. I was inspired by Hannah's faith for the child and then trust that God would take care of him when she gave him back to the temple priest. I knew I wanted a different life for my child, I just didn't quite know how to start the process. My previous behavior was falling right in line with the generational issues that plagued my family. Now I was about to become a mother, and it was a role I wasn't ready for. I read the story over and over, trying to make sense of why my granddad insisted I read this story. What I didn't realize then, was that God was showing me how my faith (like Hannah's) would be my foundation for providing for my child.

When I gave birth to my first son Kortez in 1991, I remember lying in the hospital room not knowing what to expect. I had no idea what I was in for when those labor pains hit! Everyone was so excited but in those next ten hours of labor, I really didn't see what they were so excited about. Then, I began to think of the other pregnancies that I terminated. Those children had a right to live, and I took their rights away. I thought the labor pain I was dealing with was God's punishment for aborting those other babies. During the abortions, there was some degree of pain, but it would eventually subside. Then I was back to life as usual … without a kid. Sex, alcohol, staying out late, or not coming home at all. Lying about where I was and fighting for independence from my family. But this time, there was no turning back. I fought back the constant thoughts, which I later discovered was grief and shame from aborting my children. This added to the guilt I would carry for many years.

I was still crying from so much pain after hours of labor, and that's when the nurse brought my baby to me and laid him in my arms. I looked at him and he looked at me, then we both began to cry. "Lord, how am I going to take care of this child by myself? What am I going to do?" I began to understand Hannah's faith.

My Kortez's birth saved my life because when he arrived, I had to change. There was something about this child that was different. His birth was the beginning of my slow process of healing.

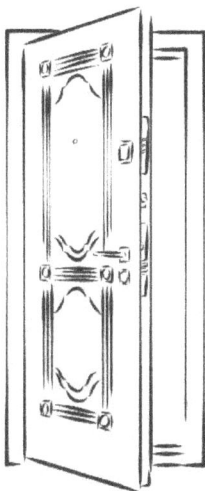

TWELVE

Sister Unforgiveness had one thing right, we had no idea how important Kortez's birth would be to mending our family back together. During this time, my grandmother, Bigma, was getting older and was starting to show early signs of Alzheimer's Disease and Dementia. Many of our family members were not speaking to each other because of unforgiveness and riffs running through the family. Kortez seemed to help mend some of those past hurts and started to bring the family together.

Day by day, it became a little easier to provide for my son because I wasn't alone. Momma was there with me. She helped us the best she could. I kept asking myself, *"Who is this lady and what have you done with my mother?"* When it came to her grandchild, she was not the same woman who raised me. She was crazy about him, as he was about her. I often felt he loved her more, but it was her patience with him that he connected with. We hear people say, "There is something about a grandparent-grandchild relationship that brings in a special type of love." He lovingly called her "Gammy," and she would melt each time he said her name. They had a special bond.

Bigma would babysit while I worked, and of course, she was compensated for her time. When she became ill and was unable to take care of Kortez, it was in those times I leaned on other family members to help. Bigma wasn't happy about this because she thought Kortez belonged to her. She tried to break down those new family connections because of their willingness to be a part of my village.

At this time, I began to understand more and more about prayer. I received a devotional Bible in a simpler translation which made it easier for me to understand the Scriptures. I also began reading other Christian materials along with self-help books.

I read several books from different female authors which brought enlightenment into how you cannot change your past yet how your past can help better your future. I was still dealing with depression but had to push through because now I had a child to take care of. I read many books growing up, it was my way to escape into the fantasy world. But these books were speaking directly to my spirit. Their accounts of their journey walked me through some crazy moments. They spoke from experience. They were willing to speak about the violence they dealt with in an abusive relationship with transparency and honesty.

Again, in the African American community, we kept everything to ourselves because it was not acceptable to speak about mental illness or abuse openly. You were deemed weak. The women in our family were all expected to be strong and focused while following the example of the generation before. Yet there wasn't an expectation on the men to raise their children and be husbands and head of households. In our family, our relationships between the women were very difficult. It didn't matter whether it was mother-daughter, aunt-niece, grandmother-grandchild, the relationships were not healthy and were difficult to follow. For example, my uncle had two children who were raised by their mothers. He was told by his parents not to give those kids his name nor to be an active part in their life because of the stigma it would bring because of who their mothers were. This is an example of the double standard between the two gender roles.

I struggled to build healthy relationships with women. I didn't have a problem with men, but women were different. I wasn't a good friend, nor did I understand how to set healthy boundaries in friendships. Either I ran my mouth about someone else's life, or I was the one being talked about. I would pick a woman I thought had it all together and work hard to get into her circle. That became my focus. It's humiliating to think of how ridiculous I must have looked trying to get in with "the cool kids!" But this wasn't just me, this was many of the female friendships I had witnessed. Unless we see healthy relationships and have an example of what it can look like, we can struggle with our own insecurities and feel either inferior or superior in our own relationships. I now see that growth comes when we just learn to live and accept each other for who we are as we grow.

As I began to study God's Word, I began to slowly get to know Him, and to understand His character. But there was still this struggle within myself to be loved and validated by those around me. I started attending a women's Bible study and conferences with my mom and other women. I noticed there was usually a woman that stood out from everyone else, quiet, and reserved. It was that woman I always ended up having a conversation with after I was rejected from the cool kids' club. She would be someone I believe was divinely placed in my presence to speak life into my situation. I didn't need to pretend with her because she was genuine in her approach and concern for others. As I think back now, I see God was showing me the type of relationship I should cultivate. It would take me some time to realize this.

My friend Shirley was that type of person. I would meet her a few years later. She didn't have a problem telling me when I was wrong and treated me like a younger sister because she was twenty-five years older. Shirley was a Godsend in my life, helping me to grow in my faith and understand that healthy relationships with other women could exist. Shirley died of brain cancer around 2000, but I still have a note she wrote to me urging me to continue in my walk with Christ. Her friendship was genuine and pure. I learned a lot about being a woman and more importantly, a Godly woman of faith. She reminded me of the woman spoken of in the book of Titus. Titus 2:3,4 says:

Similarly teach the older women to live in a way that honors God.

… These older women must train the younger women to love their husbands and their children, to live wisely and be pure, to work in their homes, to do good and to be submissive to their husbands. Then they will not bring shame on the word of God.

Shirley's voice sparked many moments of self-correction, and still does, even to this day. I thank God that He never gave up on me even when I was ready to give up on myself. His love to me was shown by placing women like Shirley in my life as a guiding light; ultimately as a reflection of Him.

THIRTEEN

Momma getting sober was a pivotal point in her life because now as she sought the Lord to be her Provider and her Savior, she didn't need the liquor anymore. It was as if she was coming out of a fog walking into a field of sunlight. By this time, she was enjoying being a grandmother to my son, Kortez. This relationship was also a reason she stayed clean because she knew that if I saw any familiar behaviors from her past, she wouldn't be in his life.

As Granddad continued to flourish as a pastor, he went back to school to earn his Bachelor's and Doctorate Degree in Divinity! How proud he was of himself, this little Black boy from the cotton fields of Louisiana, now known as Dr. Rev. Matthew Rutland, Sr. His sermons would often include stories of his upbringing and how he was called into the ministry in his pre-teen years in a shack of a church in his hometown. Granddad believed if you worked hard and trusted God, you had everything you needed. The more he flourished, the more he tried to do for his family. "Trini, (is what he called me) everything I have is for y'all. I do this for y'all. When I'm gone everything goes to my wife. Your grandma divorced me otherwise she would've had this. I can't do nothing for her. I do what I do for my family. Everything I can do, I will do while I'm living because it is for my family."

Granddad's wife was a pistol. Momma endured backlash from her like so many others that wandered into her path of rage. It was probably the alcohol and maybe a mental illness. She was a little stout lady, maybe about 170 or 180 pounds, with a creamy complexion and dark wavy hair. She could dress just as well as any other pastor's wife and she could cuss like a sailor. People often wondered why Granddad stayed with her, and why he endured what he endured from her. Momma would often say that Granddad felt guilty about leaving his first wife and was determined not to make that same mistake. When Granddad's wife wasn't drunk, she could be the most giving person you ever met. But it was her rage that was most memorable.

However, the more Momma learned of the Lord the more her heart turned towards Him. She became a devout Christian, a scholar of the Scriptures, and a woman of wise counsel. She never returned to alcohol as her coping mechanism, she turned to the Lord. Her addiction was her faith. There were relationships that came and went, but if Granddad did not approve of them, they didn't seem to last. She wanted very much to please Granddad, and I would say Bigma too.

She was still living in the same house with Bigma until around 1993 when she and a group of friends won the lottery! Momma was instantaneously a millionaire! It helped her (and me) get completely out of debt. She was now able to afford her own home in a neighboring suburb of Detroit while taking care of her mother. She also got the chance to travel a lot.

It was amazing to see this overnight transition in my mother's life. She and her friends all came out with a significant portion of the winnings, even after taxes. My mom, having opted for annuity payments, would soon find out that God would coordinate it in such a way that the deposit would hit her bank account every year on the exact date of my birthday. Momma always made sure to generously acknowledge and celebrate my birthday accordingly.

Around this time, Kortez and I moved in with the man who would later become my husband. Bigma was in her home, by herself, and was starting to show signs of dementia. Momma retired from her job of twenty years to take care of Bigma, but Bigma was soon moved to a nursing home where she could get proper care.

The separation from Bigma caused Momma to slowly begin to come to terms with her relationship with her mother. She didn't go to therapy yet started to process their relationship along with everything she endured as a child. I think had she sought professional counseling, she may have had a better understanding of the mental stress she dealt with. She continued to experience bouts of depression where the demons of her past would drive her into isolation. She suffered with this in silence because again, this is not something we talked about. She was viewed as a leader in the church, the product of her father, and therefore she didn't think she could show signs of imperfection. There were times when Momma would shut down from the world, no phone calls, and she would not answer the door, just a complete shut down for days and then she would reemerge like nothing happened. This would happen especially if I did something that was against her wishes. It was the same mind control game Bigma played with her, and she could do it just as well as her mother. Momma showed signs of depression and then denied it because her "faith" was stronger. Seeking counseling or therapy was not something she would discuss, yet I remember when she was at rehab, and therapy was a part of the program, it had helped her.

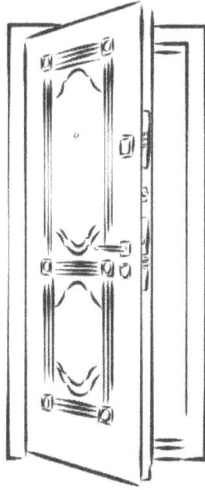

FOURTEEN

As the days turned into years, I had replaced my closet and prayer time with God with relationships with people and stuff. Life was what it was as the seasons changed into my teenage years and beyond. My ability to discern facial expressions, body language, and the room's atmosphere deepened while trying to build friendships and later (unhealthy) relationships. I honestly didn't know how to be a friend. Growing up, my only real friendships were with my brother and cousins.

Because I often had to care for myself and my brother, including making sure we ate, walking him to school and keeping a careful eye on my mom, I learned how to take charge when needed. These survival skills weren't helpful though when I was trying to make friends and engage in challenging peer pressure situations. I had a few neighborhood friends I played with, but play would turn inappropriate at times. Because of my exposure to adult behavior concerning sexuality, it seemed acceptable to experiment. I grew up in a time when everyone looked out for each other reporting any misbehavior by the kids on the block. Before I could get in the door for the night after a full summer day of play, Bigma and Momma would report back what "Miss Nosey" told them over the phone. I can't say punishment was not warranted, because it was, but the form of physical punishment could vary greatly. My mom learned her parenting skills from her mother, so the level of punishment could be extreme and severe. This was not uncommon in our community because it was expected that children would be seen and not heard. And if they misbehaved, the behavior was dealt with immediately. So, I tried very hard to find the balance between being a good child and fitting in with my peers.

As a child having to render solutions to adult problems a lot of the time, there was a fine line between understanding child and adult responsibilities. This pressure drove me to always strive to be the best.

It warranted approval from my family, praise, and their positive attention for me. In everything I did, I tried to succeed without fail. If I failed, or didn't achieve my goal, I was very hard on myself and would slip into a mood of silence. The attention doesn't come when you are not the best! My mom would say, "Be the best you can be in whatever you do. If you are a street sweeper, be the best damn street sweeper they've ever seen." I took this phrase literally and pushed myself hard. There was a lot of pressure to be the good kid to get my mom's approval. Yet it was not so easy to make friends because I didn't understand the rules and boundaries of true friendships. My ability to read others' body language and doing what I thought would please them became my formula for approval.

I think back on how much I embarrassed myself because I tried to insert myself into groups that were popular instead of finding people who liked me for me. I would leave interactions feeling unworthy, used, and depleted. The guys only seemed interested in being your "friend" until the sexual encounter was achieved. And that gave them bragging rights! Unfortunately, with a trail of bad choices as a teenager, I encountered several men in their twenties. They could understand me and appeared to appreciate my level of maturity. They gained more than they gave.

At this same time, I was active in my church. I was expected to attend church for all the services, and work in whatever ministry I was assigned. I enjoyed being at church, but the pressure of being accepted by my peers and the notion of having to be perfect was too much. I didn't understand about God's grace and definitely didn't understand how to extend grace.

The doctrine of my church was that you had to be baptized or you were going to hell. You had to attend church whenever the doors were open, or you would be deemed an unfaithful Christian. A church member's level of Christian maturity was based on how they served inside and outside of the church. There were many families in the church with children all around the same age, so we all grew up in this belief system and doctrine. I won't say it was horrible because I learned many valuable lessons. We were taught the foundation of the Baptist beliefs, and Biblical foundations like the books of the Bible, and their categories. I learned how to socialize and operate in church services along with structure and proper formality. My grandfather was all about doing things decent and in order. Because of this, he was well-respected within the Southern Christian Leadership Community and amongst the Black Baptist community.

Those times taught me many things and prepared me for when I began working at the age of sixteen. I understood the assignments and could complete them effectively. I exhibited leadership skills and would gain the respect of my peers and management with ease. My people pleasing obsession, (plus anxiety) would drive me to go above and beyond.

Yet, I still struggled with female friendships and relationships. I watched and heard how women would drag each other through the mud and then smile at each other in person. I made the mistake of opening up to a few of the women in our church looking for guidance and acceptance. Boy, was I surprised and hurt when what I shared was repeated around the church. I thought I could let Katrina share in this experience of godly female bonding because it felt genuine. After all, we were a part of the same church family. A few months in, another church member came to me about some conversations being shared about me … I just couldn't believe it! Yet, I don't know why I was surprised because this was the female culture within the congregation … smiling in your face while knifing you in the back. This cultivated a sense of distrust amongst the next generation of young women who began to stop attending church regularly. Young families weren't joining the church like the previous generation. There just wasn't the same sense of spiritual oneness within the Body of Christ. God would bring other people into my life that would show me so much godly love, but I wouldn't trust it. I couldn't trust anyone because if they knew the real me … they would turn on me like all the others.

I retreated into my own sort of protective closet; vowing never to trust anyone else again. Katrina needed to be protected because she was easily hurt, used, and manipulated. She sought validation, approval, and love but didn't know how to size up a person to see if they were good for her. Trina trusted easily and worked hard to gain others' approval despite their not so good intentions. Trust came with conditions and pain. Emotionally, I was starving for approval … affection … fulfillment. I retreated to the closet often during this period.

And then in 1992 I met Darnell.

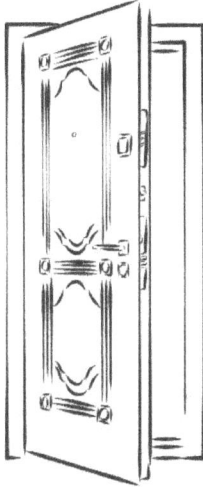

FIFTEEN

Darnell worked for the Detroit Fire Department. He was only a few inches taller than me, but muscular from weightlifting and jogging. He donned a smooth bald head and kept a clean shaved face because of his position with the department.

We met at a club, on a girls' night out for me. He had my interest from the very start. I could tell he was different. After being with many men from age fourteen to twenty-two, I could tell there was something special about this one. Darnell was very direct and would speak his mind. He was bold and confident. And I felt special and protected by him almost immediately. In fact, at the same club, an ex had shown up and was questioning me about "this guy" and if he was the reason we broke up. As I danced with my ex to placate him, one of my friends had dared Darnell to rub my leg on the dance floor. He did it! (And I liked it!) Needless to say, the ex realized it wasn't going to work out with us, so he left.

Darnell and I enjoyed spending time together at family events, work functions, and evenings out. Because he had his own home, we never had to worry about finding alone time. He was so enthusiastic about life and would oftentimes talk about big dreams, and world views. I enjoyed listening to his voice and hearing his passion for his visions. Darnell was a tough one to love because of his hardcore way of thinking and sometimes dogmatic approach to getting things done.

Since at the time we met, I had still been living with Momma, after dating for approximately a year-and-a-half, he offered his home as a refuge for me and my son. He had a little girl two years older than my son who lived with her mom. We did spend quite a bit of time together with the kids, especially when she would come over for the weekend.

I was studying the scriptures before meeting Darnell and was trying to raise my son more in accordance with Biblical teachings all while still living at home with my mom. I regularly attended Christian women's conferences and was reading various Christian books. I was searching for a deeper understanding of God, and by this time I had come to realize there was more to God than hell and brimstone. I still couldn't believe that God could forgive me for everything and wash it clean. Eventually I felt the Holy Spirit moving in my life through the teaching of some of the gifted teachers I had been reading and hearing. They inspired me to learn more about Christ for myself.

Before I made the move to Darnell's home, we sat down and had a conversation with my mom. It was important to me that I received her approval for this decision because she knew the struggle I was having with my grandmother. Darnell and my mom and I sat at the dining room table on the second floor of the two-family flat of our home. We had a good conversation about my mom's expectations of the man that I would be with for the rest of my life. I already had a child, and she was hoping that I would get married before I moved out. That wasn't the case, but it didn't change the conversation she had with Darnell. One thing she said that really stuck with him, even to this day was, "you're taking her from our home but when you are done with her you bring her back." I honestly didn't know how to feel about that. Was I a piece of meat? But it was a statement Darnell always remembered. Momma knew from her own experience, some relationships just don't work out. If that would be the case, it was clear I could always come back home.

Even though he had not expressed a desire to get married when we first hooked up or to have more children, our years being in a relationship yielded both. After getting married in 1995, we became a blended family and had two more children. It was important to him that we showed the children the world outside of Detroit. Darnell enjoyed traveling and it was one thing I really liked about him; he was very adventurous and wanted to see the world. We often took family trips to Chicago, New York, and even Jamaica.

When I met Darnell, I was ready for a new life and thought I was ready to be a wife. Boy, was I unprepared. The only examples of marriages I had were from my church, the divorces within my own family, and my dad's side of the family. I'll just say, there weren't that many I could look up to, but my paternal grandparents set a good example of death till we do part. Bigma didn't like my husband because he didn't fall in line with our family dysfunction. Even though I was married, it was expected that I put my relatives before my husband and household. As a matter of fact, as time went on, I began to put everything before my marriage and family. I was so out of order. I believed that my mom and the church knew what was best because we were Christians. My husband and I had many disagreements about my loyalty to everything else but our household. I was striving for excellence but for the wrong purpose. I thought I was really doing God's work and was praised for my strong dedication. Yet my home life was slowly turning upside down and our marriage crumbling.

Our marriage was built on love but there were also secrets that I brought into our relationship. I did not disclose to him the trauma and abuse I dealt with growing up, so he really did not know what he was getting into. I often would lie to him about things that I was doing or places I was going. Naturally that behavior became a reason for him not to trust me fully. I just did not know how to be in a healthy relationship or to be his wife. I figured sex would always answer any problems but with sex came my emotional desire. Darnell did not know how to respond to my emotional needs, and they were huge. He was a man that was focused on taking care of business, providing for the family, and making sure that we were safe. His responsibility was paying the bills, going to work, and providing for his household that was constantly growing. What he needed was a partner to support his efforts and not someone that was bent on doing her own selfish things. I must say that when times got hard, I expected him to leave, or to tell us to go, but those words never crossed his lips. The harder our relationship was, the more I expected him to turn away, but he never did ... at least physically. Emotionally though, he was shutting down. Neither of us knew how to meet each other's needs the way that the other needed it. We were speaking two completely different love languages.

I shared some of my life with a woman in the church whom I thought I could trust. (Yes, I did it again.) She came across as someone I could speak to for sound advice about marriage. She would talk with me from what appeared to be a sincere heart. I would call her when I needed someone to talk to and felt I could trust her. Until one day, when it got back to me some of what I shared with her. I don't know why I was so hurt by this action again because I did it as well ... but it hurt deeply again. I began to understand "Do unto others as you would have them do unto you." This was a practice I had to start focusing on. Slowly, my life concept began to form: "Be who you needed when you were growing up."

At this point, I was married for a few years and a mother of four. You would've thought I'd learned these lessons by now, but I hadn't. Bouts of depression were coming more and more. Momma told me I wasn't trusting God enough and needed to repent. I did. Over and over again. But the thoughts of my past would supersede the reality that God could actually forgive someone like me. How could He? How could He forgive someone who went back on their promises to Him? Someone who would lay in bed at night worrying about yesterday's mistakes and tomorrow's uncertainty? An individual who couldn't make a clear decision without second guessing her choices? Someone who was trying to be perfect and live up to everyone else's expectation while feeling so empty and conflicted within? How could He forgive me for not trusting Him? Because the bottom line was, I didn't trust Him. To be honest, I didn't really know Him. Yes, He was present, but I didn't really know Him. I judged my relationship with Him on the same level as my earthly parents. I felt I had to be perfect in order to get into heaven, and I rationalized that since I wasn't, my salvation was uncertain.

I thank God that through these tough times, Darnell and I didn't give up. He had a difficult time expressing to me his emotions and what he needed in our relationship, but slowly, we started to work together. Looking back on those moments now, I realize he was just trying to tell us he loved us by providing and being the man that he needed to be for his family.

It was important to us both that the children went to well-established schools to get the best education that we could afford within the community that we lived in. But the neighborhood was disintegrating pretty quickly, and we were worried that our boys would not make it. Our home was broken into twice while we weren't home, and we were burglarized. And then one day when Darnell was at work the children and I were home alone, and someone began to kick the side door. It was the most frightening experience I have ever gone through in my entire life, trying to figure out how to defend my home and keep our children safe. Thank God we scared the intruders away only moments before the police and the fire department arrived at our house to assess the scene. I was scared to death, and Darnell immediately went into protector mode. He secured our home. The intruders had kicked in the window of our side door, and he stayed home that night to make sure we were safe. Then the next day, he stayed home just in case the individuals returned. Wouldn't you know it they did! They were young kids from the neighborhood breaking into homes and trying to score things to sell.

But unfortunately for them they came back to the wrong house. This time as they came through the back alley and jumped the fence of our backyard, they did not know that Darnell was inside the house, waiting for them with a baseball bat! He opened the door and chased them, managing to catch one, after the others hopped the fence. Needless to say, the bat came in handy. We never had an issue again with someone breaking into our home, but that was the pivotal moment when we realized we needed to find somewhere to live that was safe for our family. We began the search for a larger home in a better community that would be suitable for our family, plus my mother-in-law. This is the way my husband always thought; take care of the family.

He did not have his father in his life to be the example of what a husband and a father should be, so he did what he thought was best. I truly believe God gives us the spouse we should have, because I don't think any other man would have put up with the issues that we had in our marriage. I'm not saying that he was a complete saint, but he always tried to do what was best, and right, and fair. So, when we began to have marital issues, he was very selective with whom he would trust to get advice from. The issues that we were having became triggers for him because of some childhood issues he had experienced. I don't want to tell my husband's story because it is not my story to tell. But I know he had a hard time trusting me because of some of the things he saw as a child, and my own actions did not help to ease his tension or give him peace of mind. So, we did the best that we could to raise our family by giving them the life we did not have. Excellent schools, summer camps, family vacations, the ability to explore all types of sports with our full support, and other school functions.

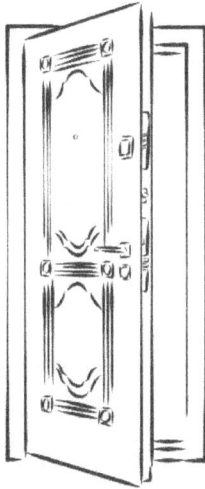

SIXTEEN

By this time, in the early nineties, my little family had grown which gave Momma much to look forward to as a grandmother. She lavished me and the grandchildren with gifts. I could tell it was her way of trying to make up for the early times in my life. The children had wonderful Christmas experiences with their grandmother, and she would oftentimes pay for trips just for me and her.

Bigma's health was deteriorating, and Granddad's health was slowly becoming worse as well. It was later determined that he was fighting prostate cancer. Momma became more devoted to her father's mission, ministry, and health, making sure he made his doctor's appointments, and any other needs. By this time, her brother was taking care of Bigma's medical needs, so Momma was able to focus on Granddaddy. It was a real strain on her, and I can only imagine the emotional toll it was taking, but she never really talked about it. Actually, she did, but she talked about all of the issues that she and her mother and siblings had. She began to speak more and more often about how she felt like she was the outcast in the relationships of mother and daughter and sibling and sibling. Momma became more reliant on my relationship with her and the relationship with our children to the point that I felt like she was inserting herself in places she shouldn't. This reminded me a lot of how she and her mother's relationship was.

In 1998, my dad suffered a massive stroke and required twenty-four-hour care. Bigma was diagnosed with Alzheimer's and dementia and was receiving care in a long term-nursing home, slowly dwindling away from the condition. She was a shell of the woman who helped raise me, very thin and frail. The feistiness was still there, but her memory of times past was gone. Whenever I visited her, it broke my heart and saddened me to see her in this condition. My mom had the chance to care for her mother but relented to the pressure from her brother who gained guardianship. I wanted my mom to fight for her mom, but she wouldn't. She felt that finally, she was out of her control. Her mother was someone else's responsibility, and she could just go visit and leave. Afterall, she took care of her mother all her life, even after she purchased her own home. She was finally free. I see that now but didn't quite understand it at the time. My aunt was in the same facility having suffered several strokes and was paralyzed on one side. Her condition deteriorated to the point of total paralysis. Sadly, within the next year both Bigma and Aunt Vera shared the same fate.

This was a difficult time in our family. Many family issues were coming to light and arising amongst our family and a lot of family secrets were starting to surface. This was about the time when my mom began to open up about her past, as well as her mother's. The abuse and trauma ran much deeper than I could have imagined, but the truth was starting to take shape. The stories were starting to ooze out like slow moving slime. Sexual abuse, humiliation, being shamed into participating in unthinkable activities for the sake of money or control. Momma began to share what really was happening in that house we lived in with Bigma. I knew she was not exaggerating because it triggered memories of scenes I witnessed as a child. Her stories came in spurts but one that stood out was an act of mystical southern practices.

Bigma would burn candles and incense in the house, but there were other artifacts around the house that were out of place. As a child, I knew not to touch certain things, but I was very curious. When Momma would tell me these stories of what was really happening during these parties, it started to make sense. Bigma would place candles under her bed and there were many times I witnessed her on her knees praying, but she wasn't always praying to the God that we knew. Specifically black candles were burned, and I could remember the tension in the house being very high. I was told this was when Bigma was focusing on a specific person for something bad to happen to them or a situation she wanted to control.

I told Momma about an errand Bigma took me on with her one day. She told me she wanted me to take a ride and we were going to visit a friend. On our way there she stopped by the bank to get some money and she also brought along items in her handbag. When we arrived at our destination, it was a little house located in the middle of the block. It appeared to be a two-bedroom home all on one level and we had to enter an aluminum fenced yard to get to the door. Once inside, an older lady about Bigma's age invited us in. We walked through the house that seemed normal; a living room with furniture covered in plastic protective covering, floor runners which we walked on through the formal dining room, and small kitchen to the right into a back hallway which led to a bedroom. In this room, there was a card table with a dark tablecloth. There was a diverse selection of candles, incense of different sizes and colors, and dark wooden artifacts on the wall. There was a green bookshelf filled with various books which reminded me of Bibles and encyclopedias. There was also a small bowl with black charcoal inside, but what I remember most were the candles in the room and the distinct smell of oils and incense that lingered in the air. I was told to sit in a chair off to the side as Bigma and this other woman, Helen, sat together at the small card table. Bigma pulled an item out of her handbag that belonged to my uncle's wife. I recognized the item, but I cannot remember exactly what it was. It was something with her picture on it, like her driver's license or work ID. I remember thinking, *how did she get that?* Now I knew that there was a lot of tension in our family in regard to my uncle's wife and their marriage. The bottom line was that Bigma did not like this woman. And because she didn't like her, that same feeling was shared by everyone else in the family.

Bigma began to tell Helen about my uncle's wife, describing her in very disrespectful words. I was used to such descriptions of other individuals. Bigma could be very vicious in her assault on someone's character because of unlikely relationships, or interactions Bigma did not approve of. Bigma told Helen that she believed a spell had been placed on my uncle by this woman during a recent trip to Mississippi, and Bigma wanted to counteract the spell. Bigma justified this visit by saying she was trying to protect her son from evil!

Helen began to create some type of mixture and lit candles as she began to talk to Bigma about what she needed to do with the mixture. I can't remember the specifics, but I do remember the woman prophesying over what would happen to my uncle and his wife. Then she began to tell Bigma about other people in our family and their fortunes. She asked Bigma if she wanted to know about me, and Bigma told her yes. Helen turned to me and said, "You will have three husbands. Your first husband will be the father of your child, but the relationship will not last, the second husband will be a short relationship. But the third husband will be the man that you will love and be with the rest of your life living in a house with a white picket fence."

I had to be about ten or eleven when this happened. It was ingrained in my mind for the rest of my life. When I shared this information with Momma, she was not surprised, but also a little upset because she had no idea that Bigma was exposing me to witchcraft to that degree. She knew exactly who I was talking about because she had been there quite a few times herself. We also figured out that Bigma was ultimately trying to groom me for the ritualistic lifestyle she had. At that age I was very sensitive to spirits in the houses of people that had passed away. I knew to go to Bigma and tell her of these encounters because she would know what to do. The interesting part about this story is that Helen would be right.

When Momma and I started having these conversations I had been married a few years. I was also running my own business in our basement for an in-home daycare. I was taking college courses for my degree in early childhood studies. I was also taking classes in psychology and child development. Through these courses, I began to understand how the brain works, the influences of outside stimuli on the body, and how a child develops. I began to learn more about how outside stimuli can directly affect the way a child develops, and the negative impact alcoholism, abuse, neglect, and trauma can have on the child's brain. I believe at this time I was slowly starting to make some connection as to why my childhood was the way it was. I started to face the issues that I was dealing with, such as depression, and how my past directly affected what I was experiencing emotionally and mentally. Even though I was starting to make the connections, the desire for approval and to please was still very deep. I began therapy to uncover how the childhood trauma I experienced was affecting my life.

Whenever the conversation about me seeing a therapist came up, Momma would quickly dismiss the conversation. She'd say all I needed was Jesus and if I needed to see a therapist, my faith was not as strong as it should be. I was told I did not trust God. If I trusted God, He would heal everything that was going on in me. This brought on a totally different level of guilt and complicated my struggle with faith in God. I knew she meant well, and that it wasn't with the intent to shame me, but that's exactly what it did. It brought on such a level of guilt that I stopped therapy and tried to do it on my own. Yet God was staying in the mix. He was making sure that I was still receiving the knowledge I needed to break through all of what I was dealing with. He was setting in motion the wisdom and education that would feed my brain to a point that I could understand why I was behaving or acting the way I was. I still did not fully understand how God could deliver me from the struggle I was having within myself emotionally and mentally to be validated and approved. I still wasn't getting it in the tangible, physical sense, and I definitely wasn't looking to get it from my dad. I just didn't understand that I could get it from God, and it would be all I needed. I didn't know, it was called grace.

I want to make something perfectly clear; I do not blame my mother at all for her efforts to be my mother. I don't hold it against her, because in all she was doing, she felt what she was doing was right. It was her way of trying to "support" me, her struggling daughter, and she didn't know how to help me. Since she and her mother had such a volatile relationship, I know now Momma was trying to do something different. Yet in her efforts to do different things, she picked up many of Bigma's traits, such as a spirit of manipulation because she knew I would do just about anything to please her. The stories Momma shared about Bigma's past also helped me understand who she was as a woman. Bigma too was violently abused as a young child.

This is how Trina felt she needed to live to survive, making sure that everyone in her space was okay. Feeling the vibes, understanding the moods, reading the room, and doing what was necessary to fix the situations. I still had that deep desire to just do what I felt others wanted me to do. I also felt I had to continue to seek out the emotional connection I needed to feel whole.

SEVENTEEN

My grandfather was getting older and was in need of help in the ministry. A minister and his family joined our church. Minister Evans began teaching Bible study, Sunday School, and preaching on Sundays. He preached in a way that many of us could understand and relate to. I believe that's when my thirst for God's Word began to expand. He wasn't all over the Bible but instead taught on specific topics and was very knowledgeable and gifted to preach to God's people. He also began to open our eyes to teachings that were not biblical or profitable for God's people. My grandfather was very grateful for his help in the ministry but guarded his position as the pastor.

Minister Evans was at our church for approximately nine months before being called back to his previous church. During that short time, my family and theirs bonded. My mom treated their daughter and son like her grandkids. Our families spent a great deal of time together. The Evans' presence was a good distraction and I truly believe they were sent to that little storefront church for several reasons including for us to build a relationship. The shenanigans in the church were becoming too much for me to witness. Granddad was being challenged continuously about the business of the ministries and I felt a need to protect him. This protective need deepened, but he would often tell his family to stand down. His exact words to me were, "Trini, I trust God. They don't think I see and know what's going on, but I do. I see it at all. I'm trusting God!" Then he would go on to tell me something he knew that he either saw or was told. It was so disheartening to watch him deal with that in the church. As much as I loved my Granddad and the church family, I needed to find a place where I could grow in the Word.

I didn't feel comfortable at my home church and joined my dear friend Shirley's church. At that church, there were a lot of older women and their women's ministry was very strong. This is where my desire for the Bible deepened even more. Through

Women's Bible studies, attending women's retreats, and learning to focus more on my spiritual growth, I learned a lot during this time.

As I stated before, my mom was very supportive of our growing family, but I think that's when her need to control me in order to stay in my life began. The relationship became stronger, as I still wanted very much to please Momma. I moved back to my family's church and worked in the various ministries dragging my kids with me. We spent a lot of time at church and at my mom's house. My husband wasn't feeling it and oftentimes arguments would erupt because of the commitment and the amount of time we were at church and away from home. Momma was okay with this because then she had more control over me, and the children and she made it out as though my husband was the enemy. She was doing the same thing to us as was done by Bigma. My husband began to withdraw emotionally, and I began to seek that attention elsewhere.

We were married for about eight years when I found myself in an emotional relationship outside of my marriage. I began to receive emotional support from someone other than Darnell. It was never physical, but emotionally it was everything I felt I needed. Trina was finally understood and accepted. I knew it was wrong, but it didn't matter ... it was almost worth the chance to be fulfilled. I even prayed for God to support these unacceptable indiscretions. My view of God and my marriage vows were all out of order. I viewed my success outside the home as a blessing, but it really was God's mercy. Trina was going on with life, doing what she wanted and accepting this false sense of fulfillment as God's blessing, but I was riding on God's mercy train and my ride was coming to an end.

My husband knew something was not right and would often say he knew me better than I thought. He was reading my body language, watching my actions, listening to my conversations on the phone, and questioning my whereabouts when I hadn't been accounted for. Darnell knew something was going on. As I continued to pray asking God to help me hide my secret, the distress on my face caused my husband to back down. But backing down caused him to resent me more and more. It was very hard for him to watch me go on as if nothing happened when all he wanted to know was "Did it really happen?"

My behavior was supported and encouraged by Momma. She was her mother, and she treated me the same way she was treated. I needed her approval along with everyone else's. I felt it was what I was called to do. The Bible was used to encourage this behavior, but it wasn't used to support my marriage. I was all out of order in my marriage, family life, and my emotional and mental state. I never sexually cheated on my husband, but emotionally yes, I did. This was very hard to admit out loud.

We hit rock bottom and began to talk about divorce. Our children were in elementary school and high school heading to college. I began to come to terms with this, because, after all, everyone else in my family got divorced. Both of our parents' marriages ended in divorce. So, what's the big deal? I would be fine without him, I kept telling myself … but my granddad's words would always come back to me. "Trina, listen to your husband, stay with your husband." I was praying for a separation. But then something happened, and my husband said he didn't want a divorce.

He wanted to work things out, but I was not hopeful because I didn't feel he would be able to "make me happy anymore." I felt that he couldn't be the source of my happiness, so I should move on. I stayed, but I prayed for answers without repenting the betrayal of my emotional ties to someone else. With this act from my husband, I should've realized God was saying "No" to my prayers and "Yes" to His plan. I continued to pray and asked God to help me hide my secret. Yes,

I did! I asked God to lie for me and make it better. My husband knew something wasn't right and he would ask me who I was emotionally attracted to, and I just couldn't tell him because I was ashamed. I would have to explain the "whys" and then he would know the real Trina. If he knew Trina, oh, he wouldn't want to be with Trina. In all of this I didn't realize that I was pushing my husband away from the church. My walk with Christ meant nothing to him because my testimony and witness was tainted with lies. He saw the true me and didn't believe Christ was in it.

By this time my mom saw what was going on, she realized it was wrong and that we were headed for divorce. It wasn't something she wanted to be a part of. I still needed to be accepted by her, but the reality of our toxic relationship was evident as it had been with her own mother. I knew I needed to pull back from her so I could focus on my marriage and my family.

While I was praying for secrecy, God was setting us up for disclosure and restoration. I didn't want to go through this hard state of our marriage. I knew this was going to be a hard journey because of my choices, I wanted to run from this. It was too hard for me, and I couldn't fix it, so I was ready to hide in the closet. It would have been so much easier to run from this relationship and my own sinful actions. But

God wouldn't let me. He touched the heart of my husband to fight hard for our marriage and he did!

EIGHTEEN

God began sending women into my life who would speak life into my marriage and into me. Mrs. Caston was one of those women. She had been one of my sons' piano teachers. I had not spoken to her in a few years because she was caring for her ailing husband of forty years. He had recently passed away when she called me early one morning while I was on my way to work.

"Mrs. Stewart, this is Mrs. Caston. I just called to tell you not to leave your husband." I was floored. How did she know? I had not talked to her in several years. But God knew. My heart shook and I began to cry. I had to pull over so I could listen to her voice. She took her time when she spoke, but there was something in her tone. It was full of love for the man she missed so dearly that now was at home with the Lord. "I would give anything for him to be with me right now, even through all the illness, and the marital issues, and other stuff, I still miss him. Mrs. Stewart, you go home and be a wife to your husband." That was God speaking through this eighty-something-year -old woman. She was divinely used to showcase this eye-opening opportunity to trust Him amid the fear and the lies of the enemy. You see, the enemy was telling me I didn't deserve this type of treatment. Darnell had cut himself off emotionally, so I should do the same and let it go. Mrs. Caston's words stopped me in my tracks, and we began marriage counseling.

We somehow ended up at North Rosedale Baptist Church, sitting in front of the associate pastor who worked with couples to provide spiritual guidance and marital counseling. We sat in front of his desk and began to share everything that brought us to this point. Now I knew this was God's plan because my husband wasn't a religious man, yet we were taking directions from a pastor neither of us knew.

Pastor listened intently to everything we both had to say, then he told me to open a Bible to

Ephesians; the fifth chapter and the twenty-second verse and read it out loud. "Wives, submit yourself to your own husband as to the Lord" (ESV). As soon as the words escaped my lips, tears welled up in my eyes. I felt so ashamed and guilty because I was listening to everyone but my own husband. Darnell was looking from the outside in. He saw what the church demanded of me and our family to be considered a faithful servant. And it was actually manipulating our willingness to serve. It was also an opportunity for me to receive the emotional fulfillment that I was seeking.

In churches, members were often expected and guilted into attending every church service, no matter day or time, and were also expected to be working in the church. And in my case my kids sang in the choir, played the piano and participated in a lot of church events. My husband and I had many heated discussions about the amount of time spent out of the home for church. He saw it for what it was, mental games. So, while we sat in the pastor's office, the pastor leaned back behind the desk while Darnell and I spoke sitting across from him. The tears wouldn't stop flowing and Darnell reached over to touch my hand to comfort me. This was a brand-new interpretation of the scripture and God clearly opened my understanding. Wow, God! You mean I am out of order in Your Word! I clearly thought my service to You was exactly what I was supposed to be doing while listening to the leaders of the church. I was blown away, devastated, and hurt.

Darnell wasn't off the hook himself; he had to read Ephesians 5:25, "husbands love your wives, just as Christ also loved the church and gave himself for her" (NKJV). Pastor proceeded to explain what the scripture meant in the context of marriage, and in our marriage. I was supposed to work with my husband as his partner, his wife. Because of the first sin by Adam and Eve, it was in a woman's nature to go against the agreement or submission to her own husband. As well, husbands are being told to love their wife. This is something husbands will struggle with, but because of the strength and grace of God, we can both get through this and grow together. Pastor made jokes to lighten the mood by telling us about his marriage and the struggles he and his wife had during over thirty years of marriage. Darnell and I were in our thirteenth year and he explained how we were still young in our relationship and ability to love and live as one. We needed this. We both came from divorced families so this was a new way of looking at each other.

When we walked out of the church and into the bright sunlight of that summer day, Darnell walked up to me and hugged me tight. "I'm sorry," he said "but this was the only way I could get you to see what

I've been talking about. You don't think of anything but church, everything is church. I want you to think for yourself." I cried so hard. Oh, yes I was mad at him because he disclosed something I thought was only between us and I was angry because I had been deceived and led to believe the church was the answer to everything. Yet, what I was starting to see, was the church wasn't the problem. The problem was I put the church before my relationship with Christ, my husband, and our family. There was an idol in my life, and it was a church and the work I was performing in the building for the recognition of others. My service wasn't unto God, it was unto man. That day is still in my mind as if it was yesterday.

Despite this new understanding, Darnell and I still talked about divorce off and on, with the pastor. I still had my mind made up, but Darnell looked at things differently. During this phase in our marriage, we were also looking to move into a larger home. My mother-in-law was planning to move with us, but I wasn't sure if we would still be together.

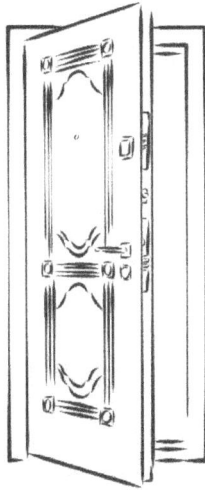

NINETEEN

My closet at this time, was a small room right off the bathroom on our second floor of our home that I shared with my husband and four children. We converted this room into a walk-in purse room. I had a deep obsession (and still do) with designer purses. So, my husband installed hooks and shelves into this small room with green walls and a door leading out onto a small back porch. I bought a vanity table and a filing cabinet where I could keep my poems, short stories, and important paperwork. This room was roughly double the size of my small closet at my grandmother's house. There was a window in the porch door and bright lighting from the light fixture which hung above the vanity table. I could sit in this room for hours and just write. It also gave me a space to get away whenever I needed to retreat into myself. Everyone knew this was my room, and not to bother me while I was in there, but they didn't know that I would retreat when the depression set in. Along with the words came the tears and darkness which would engulf me, swallowing up the peace that was trying to come in. There were handwritten scriptures taped to the wall and several Bibles in different translations on the shelf, but that seemed unremarkable compared to the darkness I clung to. Very few people knew about my experience with depression. I never told my husband because I believed he wouldn't understand.

I can only describe my survival through it all by the constant reminders that I wasn't alone. In my grade school years, I distinctly remember singing a song for our fifth-grade promotion ceremony which talked about how we would never walk alone. When I recently heard this song, it immediately triggered all types of feelings and emotions of survival. I remembered that song sparking a desire to live. It gave me a feeling that I couldn't explain; a belief and a hope that I would somehow overcome what I was dealing with. I loved to read and write poetry, so I'm not surprised the Holy Spirit used this song to touch my soul. I believe He used this song and its important words to speak within that little ten-year-old girl's heart, "You will overcome." It was only by the grace of God that I just knew deep down that I was going to be alright. That everything I was going through wouldn't destroy me because I wasn't alone. I believe the Holy Spirit was strengthening me through that song and reassuring me that He would be with me every step. Deuteronomy 31:6 says,

So be strong and courageous!
Do not be afraid and do not panic before them.
For the LORD your God will personally go ahead of you. He will neither fail you nor abandon you.

I can't remember if I was disappointed from a broken promise, or struggling with childhood life, but I felt His peace. His goodness has followed me in many forms all these years.

Looking back, we all needed therapy. Momma felt Jesus was enough. Granddad encouraged her to seek God and the church and reassured her that everything else would be okay. She joined another ministry led by a prominent female air personality. I can say, once Momma began to travel, attend spiritual retreats, and became more active in this ministry, she was more alive. She sought counsel and direction from these spiritual leaders. It was an eye-opening experience for her since, previously, she had only been a part of Granddad's congregation. With this spiritual awakening came much revelation, Biblical studies, and a greater understanding of a relationship with God. Momma was a very smart and serious student, and the Bible became her textbook. For once in her life, she was valued as a beautiful woman of God. But even in godliness, her past would continue to rear its head from time to time.

In 2005, my grandfather suffered a stroke. He too was moved to the same facility as my grandmother and aunt. He and my grandmother were together again, which was all he wanted since they had divorced some forty years prior. He was unable to talk or walk but recognized us all. Then he suffered a second stroke and was placed into hospice care at a local hospital. This was very hard for me. I loved my granddad dearly because he was that strong constant in my life. He loved me so much and was always there for me once we built a relationship.

My husband and I went to see him the night before he died. Looking at him, laying in that bed, I saw peace on his face. He was finally at peace. I promised him I wouldn't forget our talks and all the wisdom he shared with me over the years. I thanked him for taking care of me and my mom despite his limited abilities. I much appreciated the fact that he stepped into a fatherly role in my life and was a grandfather and great-grandfather in every sense of the word.

He passed away in his sleep. I was crushed.

My grandfather's passing was the first of five deaths within a twelve-month period. Bigma passed away about a month later. My uncle became extremely ill and died about six months later, and then my aunt died within a few weeks. Later that summer, my dad died while receiving care in a nursing home for a broken hip. Of all the transitions in our family, my grandfather's death affected me the most. I had never felt that level of pain before and it almost seemed impossible to endure.

I always read a lot and wrote a lot. During this time of deep loss in our family, following a prompting by the Holy Spirit, I had bought a beautiful brown leather-bound journal. When I saw it at the Barnes and Noble Bookstore, it was a must have. I remember sitting in my closet at the vanity table, gazing out of the window of the porch door. I felt this urge within me to use this journal for a new chapter in my life. During this writing session, the urging was strong to speak of the visions that I was having. Although ours was a beautiful, spacious home, I've always desired to experience more in life than what I was seeing at the time. Looking back on it now, I believe I was testing God to see if He would really answer this prayer. There was definite doubt, but at the same time, my faith was saying it is possible. So, I journaled my future home for our family. I listed it in detail:

- Four to five bedrooms
- Family room
- Library
- Finished lower level with kitchen (day care?)
- Living room
- Dining room
- Kitchen with island
- Master bedroom with two walk-in closets
- Master bathroom with double sinks
- Sunken tub with jets, walk-in separate shower
- Large backyard
- Circular driveway
- Larger foyer with closet
- Front double doors
- Enclosed patio with temperature controls
- Two to three car garage
- Mother-in-law suite
- Central air

Then I detailed room by room what I would like in this new home. I had no idea that less than a year later we would be on the path to purchasing this exact home.

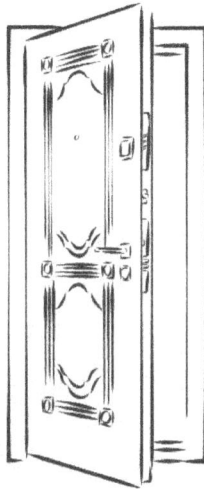

TWENTY

You expect your parents to die before you, but you do not expect your siblings to also go within the same time frame, leaving only you here. Momma would often talk about how she felt God left her here for a specific reason and it had a lot to do with carrying on what her father wished of her and being there for her grandchildren. This drove her passion to become more committed to the church ministries and to embed herself in her children and grandchildren's lives. Unfortunately, I saw Momma taking on more of those manipulative characteristics of her own mother to control anyone she could, especially me. We were very close, yet there were times when it was obvious that she wanted me and my children to be reliant on her and to disregard my marriage.

I would follow what my mother would ask of me because of the fear I had of her and my strong desire to please her at any cost. Her personality was as strong as her mother's. As much as she would say she didn't want to be like her, she was. She did not fight me, like Bigma, but it was more of an emotional attack. As I look at it now, I see it was because she needed something to hold on to; we were her family and the closest she'd ever felt to real love. We loved her unconditionally, especially her grandchildren, but her love for me always came with a price. I didn't understand my fear of her then, but I do understand it now.

We were taught to *fear the Lord.* Fear as in afraid of what can be done to you or being sent straight to hell. I equated the physical fear of my parent with the physical fear of God. I grew up afraid of what was coming next. I was always afraid of people's reactions, including Momma. There are memories even now, of indescribable scenes where my entire young body would quiver with fear at the sound of her footsteps coming towards my room, as I was told to stay there and await a very vulnerable, very traumatic punishment for my latest misdeed.

Later, I would often write Momma letters and describe some of the scenarios I remembered as a child, just to explain to her and hopefully help her understand the real struggles I still dealt with. She would read the letters or if the conversation was face to face, she would say, "Trina I don't remember, and I'm sorry. It was the alcohol and Bigma's influence on me." (As if that was supposed to make everything better.) I would say, "Momma, I think I need to go to counseling, I think I need therapy. I believe I am truly dealing with depression," and her response was always the same. "You don't trust God enough; you need to trust God more."

Her love for me was real. I have no doubt about that. But oftentimes it came with strings, and it was conditional, and it could be limited. As a child I learned how to deal with that, I would pivot to whatever I needed to do in order to keep her happy and please her. Yet as an adult, a wife, a mother, I knew I did not want to pass the same traits on to my own children. I also knew that my marriage would not stand if I continued to let her intervene.

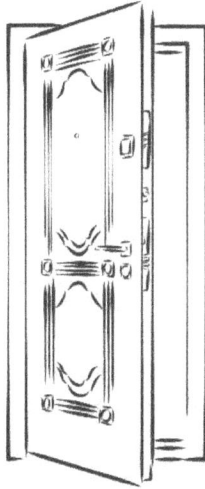

TWENTY-ONE

I began working at the YMCA as the after-school coordinator at my youngest kids' elementary school and closed the home business. A co-worker of mine was selling their family's home in Highland, Michigan and asked if my family would be interested in looking at their home. She knew about the break-ins, and we spoke about our desire to move. I had no idea where Highland was and couldn't imagine moving far from Detroit.

It was approximately one hour from Detroit. We drove out to the house at night. And as we drove, our conversation started out pleasantly but there was an elephant in the room. What were we doing? Looking for a larger home, but at the same time barely speaking to each other? I couldn't decide if my marriage was worth holding onto because I still wasn't getting the emotional attention I longed for. It would come in spurts then he would withdraw into himself leaving me confused as to where we were. I felt a longing to be loved in a different way and on my own terms. I always wanted to receive that attention and feel a deeper acceptance and love. Before I was married, I knew how to satisfy that longing by being promiscuous but then they would get what they wanted and leave. I would be left high and dry until the next call. To me, Darnell was treating me the same way, but within himself, he was battling whether he could trust me. Could he trust me with his heart and give it to me again? It would be some years later before he would open up to share the truth, that he couldn't trust me. Within myself, I took his actions as inconsistent, and unstable affection; exactly what I was used to from everyone else that I had been in a relationship with.

My husband is an amazing husband, father, provider, friend, protector, and lover. Truthfully, he was all these things then, but I honed in on my personal, and yes, selfish needs, without giving him what he truly needed from his wife. I wasn't willing to be completely honest and was afraid of his rejection. I prayed and asked God to conceal my life because I didn't want to talk about it. I even tried to barter with God. "God if you hide this, I'll never do it again." He didn't give me an answer, so I kept walking in fear, lies and distrust that God would provide either way. Yet He did give me an answer found in Proverbs 3:5-6:

Trust in the Lord with all your heart, and do not lean on your own understanding. In all your ways acknowledge Him and He will make straight your paths.
(ESV)

At this time, I was approximately forty years old, yet still having a hard time learning how to lean into God as my Daddy as a parent taking care of His child and providing for them. I looked at Him and considered that He was loving me only when I was doing right. He was working to embrace me with agape love, fatherly unconditional love, where I was looking at Him in the philo love ... which was limited love. This is the love Trina was used to because it came with rejection and judgment. Yet God was starting to show me who I really was, Katrina, His daughter *whom He loves.*

As we drove around a curve to get to the house, I could tell this was where we needed to be. We pulled up into the driveway and the house was lit with outdoor lighting as well as the lights inside the home.

There was a huge front yard with beautiful flowers and as we walked up to the door, I could see a chandelier hanging inside above the front door in the foyer. It was something I always wanted in my home. When the homeowners opened the door and we walked into the foyer, we were met with beautiful wooden floors. The living room was straight ahead with very high ceilings, a carpeted area, and a marble fireplace. I always wanted a fireplace in my living room. To our left were stairs that led up to the children's bedrooms and as we went up the steps and turned onto the first landing, there sat a desk and chair for the children to do their homework. There was an open space for the children to spend time with friends. There were three bedrooms with one shared bathroom and each room had its own unique design. Our children were currently sharing bedrooms, and this would provide the option for everyone to have their own space! We went back down the stairs to the first level and directly across the stairs was the library. I always wanted a library, and Darnell talked often about having a space where he could work. We turned to our left and walked towards the living room and directly to our right was the master bedroom. A huge opening welcomed us with an accent wall of a beautiful mauve color and the rest of the room in an off-eggshell white.

There was ample space for a king-sized bed, and other bedroom furniture as well as a master bathroom and two walk-in closets. I was floored as I walked through the home. Seeing the kitchen, the powder room, the mudroom with the attached three-car garage and finally the mother-in-law suite downstairs, my heart began to plead: "Lord, if it be Your will, let us get this home."

When we left, we had so many questions in our minds. *How can we afford this home? It was twice as much as what we were approved for. It's an hour's drive from our current location. What about the school district? And how would our children fit in, in a predominantly White area?* I kept feeling that this was the place, but without answers, we went home and continued with our life as best we could.

The phone rang about two months later, and it was the homeowners in Highland. They were willing to accept what we were approved for and knew that this house belonged to us! They built this house from the ground up specifically for their own family and now were willing to give it to us for less than they were asking for. How could this be? It was only God! I was praying for God to give me signs on which direction He wanted our lives to go. I recognized this as His divine direction to not only get our children out of the crime-ridden city of Detroit, but also to save our marriage. His direction came through this amazing blessing.

Truthfully, I was in doubt that we were going to make it in our marriage, yet God continued to bless us with everything we needed to stay together. We moved in approximately sixty days later, my husband and three of our children. Our oldest daughter was attending college and the second oldest was in his senior year of high school. My mother-in-law moved in with us as well, but for health reasons moved back to Detroit to live with her daughter later.

No one else in my family owned anything close to this and I had the audacity to believe this was possible! I remember sitting in our old home in Detroit a few weeks before getting this new home and hearing the Lord say: "Be faithful over these few things and I will bless you with much more." I got up at that moment and cleaned our entire home with a spirit of gratitude and praise. This new home represented a shift in our family's trajectory!

This was how things would always happen in my life. Employment opportunities would come as if the position was created for me in when I didn't have the required qualifications. Our family's necessities would come from unlikely sources. God just always seemed to show favor despite the craziness I was doing in my life. I honestly didn't think I deserved a home this beautiful!

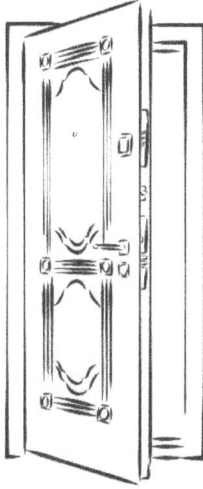

TWENTY-TWO

There we were. An hour from the closest relative, in the middle of a new city, just us. I felt as though God was setting us up for something because we had no idea how we were going to afford this home, utilities, family and maintain in a new community. Plus, we were still dealing with our marriage and conflicts in staying together. Eventually, my husband told me, "We've made it through everything else, we can make it through this." And you know what, Darnell was right.

We had the best neighbors anyone could ask for, who became a part of our family and brought us into theirs. Our kids were thriving in their new schools yet struggling in being a minority in the population. But that never stopped them from participating in every club or sport they wanted to. It was all a part of God's plan that we were to learn to trust God to sustain us while living in Highland. It was also where I broke away from the family church. There was a church split and my mom followed the new pastor. I couldn't follow her; it wasn't in my spirit to do so. For several months, we looked for a new church for our family but eventually stopped looking. We couldn't find a place we both agreed upon, so for almost a year, I went without a church home. Let me just say, I didn't miss a beat. God blessed me in such a different way. During this time, I began to see how much I was misguided in my thoughts of the church. God would show me the real Church in action when I needed it most.

The trouble in our marriage still hadn't been rectified or healed. Darnell's lack of trust in me was becoming more and more evident. It would spill over into conversations and marital interactions. I felt as though he hated me, but I couldn't give up on us because he fought so hard for our marriage. At this point, I was still praying for God to cover my indiscretion so that I wouldn't have to admit to my husband what I did. I realize now with me not trusting God and fearing my husband's reaction more, it put a huge strain on our marriage. Then we met the Lee Family.

Jamie and Joy Lee were one of several families that we immediately connected with. Ours was a community with mostly two parent households. I really liked seeing that as the normal way of life. My husband and I both worked hard at our marriage for the sake of our children because we wanted them to have the benefit of both parents in the house. And that's something that connected us with the Lees. They talked about being Christian counselors and wanted to start a ministry for marriages. I even attended one of the Bible studies held in their home. I was grateful to have these neighbors close by. They were a source of light.

The darkness in my home though was growing, especially within me. I'd spoken to my doctor about the thoughts and feelings I had been experiencing, including feelings of depression since the age of twelve or younger, and how I would say to myself, *If I wasn't here everyone else would be better off. If I leave now, then my family, my husband, my mom, and our children wouldn't have to worry about me disappointing them over and over again.* Like several other times before, I thought of taking my life. This time I didn't attempt it but there were other times.

My doctor told me that there were prescriptive ways to overcome it, including sleeping pills and antidepressants for starters. She also recommended that I see a therapist for support. I had tried therapy before but there were many stigmas around it for me. Admitting to someone that I was seeking therapy meant there was something wrong with me. It meant that there was something wrong with those around me and that there were issues. It also meant that someone else would feel as though I was blaming them and that wasn't the case, I just wanted the pain to stop. I wanted the pain to go away even if it meant I had to take my own life.

My doctor was so sympathetic to my condition. The sleeping pills weren't effective because I could wake up at the sound of the wind against the house or the frogs croaking in the pond outside my bedroom window. There were nights I could wake up from a sleeping pill as if I didn't take anything with all types of thoughts running through my head. *Should I call so-and-so to make sure they were okay with what I said earlier today? Did I handle this situation correctly? Maybe I didn't … Who is mad at me? …* The stuff that ran through my head with the emotions to match was incredible. When I eventually fell asleep, I would wake up drained!

One night, while Darnell was at work, I began to feel like everything in my life was falling apart. It was bad. Our kids were upstairs, and I was in my closet laying on a pile of clothes crying and screaming into the clothes asking God to take my life. I was in such a bad place spiritually, emotionally, and physically that I could not bring myself to get off the floor. I don't know what triggered me that day, but I could not bring myself out of this dark cloud of guilt, shame, condemnation, hurt, and pain. I was ready to take my life. I believed everyone would be better off without me. I would not be here anymore and therefore they could live their lives and be in a better place. As I laid there on the floor, I could hear the TV in the other room. A woman was on, and I could hear her giving her testimony of how she was sexually abused by her father for so many years. I'd heard her story many times before, but this was the first time it really connected, especially when she said she learned to call out in the name of Jesus. So, ever so softly, I began to whisper His name, "Jesus, Jesus, Jesus…" Over and over again and as I said His name, I felt a little stronger. I got to the point where I could get up, walk to the bathroom, and look in the mirror.

In reflection, I believe God went ahead of me and prepared the path I would take through my life. He showed me in a vision a few years ago, how angels protected me in the worst moments from the enemy's attacks. It was in my vulnerable moments like this closet experience where God kept a hedge around me. I thought, in some instances, I was ready to give in and take my life. It was in those situations God would dispatch an angel to minister to me in a way I would recognize as Him.

When sitting in that closet, the voice on the TV was that angel speaking to my spirit. Soon after, my friends Lynn and Joy became angels who would minister to my soul. 1 Peter 5:7 says, "Cast all your anxiety on Him because He cares for you" (NIV). God gave me plenty of opportunities to experience His peace. I remember reading another scripture with a clear understanding that peace came from God. 2 Thessalonians 3:16 says, "Now, may the Lord of Peace Himself give you peace all times and in every way. The LORD be with all of you" (NIV). God gave me plenty of opportunities to experience His peace.

That night I felt I needed to talk to someone, and the Lord placed Lynn in my heart. Fortunately, she answered the phone, and we began to talk. I never admitted to Lynn why I called her, but it was almost as if she already knew. She began to speak, and it was what I needed to hear. She ministered to my spirit and with words of meditation and scripture. I can't remember how long we spoke, but I felt much better by the time the call ended.

Next, Joy, my neighbor, came to my mind and I contacted her asking if we could talk. Without hesitation she cleared her schedule, and I was able to go the next morning to speak with her. When I walked in the door she looked right into my eyes, and I immediately began to cry. She held me and said, "It's gonna be okay, Trina, we're gonna get through this together." We went into her office where I sat on her couch for the next hour or two.

Joy's office was cozy. The room was decorated in earth tones with a desk, office chair, and a small loveseat. Family pictures were hung on the wall, as well as inspirational quotes. The bookshelf contained a variety of books including Bibles. Joy's voice was soft and warm as she said, "Trina, let's start with prayer." As she prayed, the tears began to flow down my cheeks and when I opened my eyes, Joy was looking intently into my face with so much compassion as she handed me a box of tissues. I asked myself, *What are you doing? She will not be able to understand what you've been through. How could she? You come from totally different backgrounds ... you from Detroit and her, someplace out here, away from the world where you've lived.* I now know, that was the enemy trying to get me to hold back, not to disclose those deep secrets and unspeakable actions I had committed in my life. *Hold back,* I could hear the voice say, … *She will not like you if she finds out this about you. She will think you are a whore and unworthy to be in her home anymore.* Man, the thoughts were coming. Yet I opened my mouth and started from the beginning.

I told Joy about my whole life, the good, bad, and ugly. She listened and cried with me at times but didn't interrupt me. She never once expressed condemnation of my life choices or judgment. I was able to be transparent and open … it felt so good to just finally get everything out. Knowing Joy was a believer in Christ, I was worried she would begin to point out my mistakes like others did many times before. She didn't. Instead, there was this soft voice telling me how much God loved me despite my faults. I answered, "How could He love me with all of the mess of the life I've led?" Joy handed me a Bible so I could read for myself, the story of His Love.

This was a first for me! Other Christian women I shared some of my life with either told me about my faults with condemning expressions or betrayed my trust by sharing my story with others. This was the one of the first times I felt supported, accepted, and loved by another Christian woman.

Joy listened ever so quietly, only asking questions to get a clear understanding of what I was saying. We talked, it seemed forever, but it was maybe an hour or so when I finally wound down. I was drained, yet relieved. Joy didn't appear shocked or surprised by what I said, in fact, she could relate to some points. She listened ever so sweetly, and she was so empathetic. She told me that she understood some parts of what I said more than others. Her eyes were eyes of love, understanding, and compassion. She started putting words to what didn't happen in my childhood, specifically, that I didn't have a regular childhood. I was focused into carrying adult responsibilities. Then she did something I could never forget, she apologized. She apologized on behalf of those people that hurt me. She apologized to little Trina sitting in the closet scared out of her mind because of the sounds coming from under the closet door. Her apology broke through the arguments from the drunkards in the living room and the yelps escaping my mother's mouth from the hard smacks being delivered to her face and body. Her apology penetrated that small closet with the chipped blue paint on the walls, and the small pile of clothes and toys on the floor where Trina would try to disappear. The pain began to resurface with these memories, but this time, it was different. This time, in the presence of love, Katrina was safe.

As we sat there, Joy again turned to the Bible for our reference, turning to the first chapter of James. She encouraged me to write down my path, starting with James 1:2-4:

Dear brothers and sisters; when troubles of any kind come your way, consider it an opportunity for great joy. For you know that when your faith is tested, your endurance has a chance to grow. So let it grow, for when your endurance is fully developed, you will be perfect and complete, needing nothing.

During our conversation, Joy said she was willing to break all my issues down and help me through them. She said she was willing to walk with little Trina to process what had happened in her childhood. She used God's Word to explain how we would get through all of it and how I could even come off the medication. As we closed out our session, she told me to begin reading the book of James and journal what God was saying to me.

I felt myself gaining some control over my thoughts and emotions. Katrina knew what to do ... she could trust Joy to walk through this journey with her. I found comfort that morning. She encouraged me to take all the time I needed to process my memories from my childhood, knowing there was nothing that could happen to me now. I was safe ... safe in God's arms because He would bring me through it all. Katrina felt as though God was answering little Trina's prayers in the closet from those many years prior. He was going to conquer the enemy in her mind, and finally free her.

This began my journey into healing from sexual and emotional abuse, depression, neglect, humiliation, shame, church hurt, the complex relationship with my mother, and in trying to root in my identity as my husband's wife, and our children's mother. It was one of the few times another woman actually showed me unconditional love. This began Trina's journey out of the closet, so that Katrina could finally come to life.

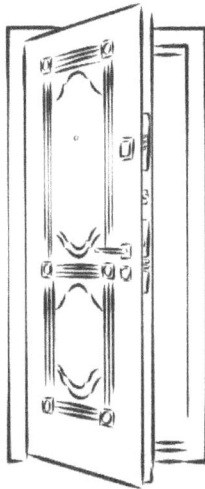

TWENTY-THREE

I viewed our home in Highland as our sanctuary. It was an hour away from any of our friends and family. It gave us the space we needed to have our alone time but still be together as a family. It represented so much within our family because it was a breaking point generationally. We had moved outside of our comfort zone to a beautiful, spacious, expensive community that wasn't surrounded by our own. We could take steps everyone else was afraid to take for the sake of our children and future generations. We were saying, "In order to live our dreams, we had to come out of the ordinary way of thinking, settling for what's convenient." We worked hard to maintain our home and become a productive part of our community. It wasn't always easy being the only African American family at our children's school events, but I started to realize we had more in common than I thought. While at a neighbor's home for a subdivision cookout, stories were shared about the difficulties with parenting teenagers, or marital issues. We all lived in these beautiful 5000 or more square foot homes with five bedrooms, and acreage behind our homes, but we all were dealing with the same family dynamics. I realized everyone was just trying to make it as best they could. We just went about it differently based on our family values and priorities.

We bonded with a core group of about six couples whom we still count as family to this day. Their genuine friendships helped pull us into Friday night card games, chartered bus trips to downtown Detroit for gambling and dinner, or spontaneous gatherings in a random driveway with music, conversation, jokes, and lots of adult beverages. I believed God was creating opportunities for us to be His Light and to receive His love from people we ordinarily wouldn't have connected with.

This new home also represented restoration from my past. I didn't know it at the time, but God was showing me how much He wanted for us to enjoy life with a spirit of praise for Him, knowing He would do the impossible for us because He loved us. It wasn't anything we had done to deserve it; it was His gift because we were His children. Looking back, I am in awe of how God touched so many lives through us while in Highland. Not only was our family affected, but complete strangers would tell us how much we inspired them to go out of their comfort zone. "If you guys can make it out here, so can I." I wanted our children to know they didn't have to settle for what life was offering, but to dream big dreams knowing God will answer according to His will. His will was for our family to live in this home for ten years! I honestly didn't think we could afford it, yet we never went without. We may not have always had what we wanted, but we always had what we needed, even if it came from complete strangers.

During one of the neighbor's parties, I was asked if we wanted to take any of the food home because there was so much food left over. I immediately said no out of embarrassment and pride. Even though we didn't have much in our pantry or refrigerator, my thinking was that since we were the only Black family at these parties, I didn't want it to appear as if we were taking handouts. The hostess wasn't hearing it. She said, "Trina, you have three kids, two of which are boys. They can eat this food within hours! Boys eat a lot! Besides, our girls eat like birds, so it's just going to go to waste." She said it with the most sincere tone, packed up the food, and told the kids to take it home. That food fed our family for the next two days. It was moments like this where I saw God taking care of us—we just had to receive it.

Another time our subdivision had a sub-wide yard sale. It was during the day, and I could not participate or attend because I was working. My kids were always in need of new clothes. Our neighbors called me over to see if we wanted anything. Again, I said "no" out of pride, but she wasn't hearing it. She started pulling items with tags on them from the piles off the table. She said, "These will fit your daughter because we are all the same size. Listen, the people that come through here are gonna pick over this stuff. Take it because I know she will like them." When I showed my daughter, she was so excited. Another God wink in a moment of need.

Our home was such a blessing because the change in trajectory was not only for my family's future but for my own. It's where Katrina began to strengthen her faith and mind. Depression had such a hold on my life until it physically hurt. I suffered from asthma, migraine headaches, fluctuating weight loss and gain and tremendous back pain. (I fell down a flight of steps as a teenager and landed on my back.) I wanted so much to please everyone I felt was important to my life that I almost lost all sense of who I was. My mom would get so mad at me because I tried hard to be friends with everyone. She told me time and time again, "When people show you who they are, believe them. Stop trying to be everyone's friend, they are not yours and don't mean you well." I would learn this lesson the hard way, would get my feelings hurt, again, and then I would slide into a period of depression that could cripple my life and my obligations to my family. Slowly, I started to see my position in others' lives and how God was using me to be the person I needed when I was growing up.

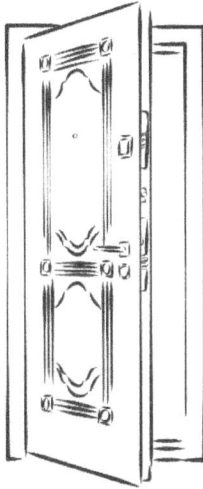

TWENTY–FOUR

I joined Minister Evan's church and while worshiping one Sunday, I clearly felt I needed to spend some time with my mom. I had previously pulled back from her because we disagreed on the religious doctrine she was following. We spoke on the phone but not as frequently as we normally would and when I did go to visit her, she was rarely alone. There was a point when she basically would seek permission before traveling, visiting friends, or communicating with others. The judgment she had for others because of their lifestyle or the way that they worshiped God was too much for me to deal with. I had come to a point where I wanted to have this beautiful relationship with my mother, but instead of it being the alcohol that was in the middle, now it was a religion.

To others, she was this beautiful woman full of wisdom and godly knowledge, including expounding on the scriptures almost as well as her dad. I will never take that away from her because that was true, she really dug into the Bible in such a profound way. That gift was only of God. Yet in her delivery, as with many religious leaders, came judgment and condemnation which she had no trouble sharing, as she did not believe in holding back. After her immediate family died, she pulled away from other family members as well; sometimes lashing out at them because of past history or just because of who they were. She and I had very different opinions about how to engage with individuals. I would first consider if the person knew Christ or not, and their need for grace. She looked at them based on what she believed was their level of salvation and if they would support her religious beliefs.

On this particular Sunday, I left my service and went to hers. I waited in the foyer for her to come out because the service was ending. I did not go in, even though my presence would bring her great pleasure, but also unwelcome attention from the other church members. I chose not to join their church so there was an unwanted pressure when I would visit.

My mom was the church secretary and treasurer, so she had responsibilities after church that she had to attend to before leaving. But, on this particular Sunday after dismissal, she saw me, ran up to me and hugged me. As I wrapped my arms around my mother, something wasn't right. She was always a small woman, but after she stopped drinking, she managed to gain and keep weight on. When I hugged her, I felt the thinness of her frame I had never felt before. It really shocked me that she was so small and reminded me of when she was younger. I said, "Mom, I came to take you out to lunch." She immediately grabbed all her belongings, told them she was leaving and walked out to the door with me hand in hand. She said, "Normally I would have to stay to take care of church business but today they're going to have to handle it themselves." It was one of those rare moments she showed an immediate desire to be with me.

Since fully joining this church and becoming one of its prominent members, she put her responsibilities first and foremost before anything else, including spending time with her family and engaging with us as a mom or a grandmother. Typically, during our time together there was always going to be a curveball. There seemed to flow in the background a constant insistence on how we could connect with her church or pastor or the ministry to grow their small congregation. And then sometimes during our time together she would call and check in, leaving, if need be, to get back to her religious obligations. So, for her to drop everything that day and walk out the door with me was huge, but I also recognized it as being something the Holy Spirit wanted me to see. We went to Applebee's for lunch.

The waitress sat us down in a small booth and for the first time I looked into my mother's face. What I saw almost shook me to my core. Her face was very thin, her frame was frail, and her eyes were huge. I asked her, "Mom, are you okay? You look a little small like you've lost weight?" she replied, "Yes I'm fine." in her normal strong "I got it all in control" voice. "I just have not had an appetite to eat lately, but I'm glad we are having this time together." She ordered a chicken Caesar salad without dairy which was something I knew she would enjoy, but she could barely eat a quarter of it. That was red flag number two. We continued through lunch and I had already decided that I was not going to internalize any judgment or condemnation that she passed on from other people and their lives or the religious tone that was in her voice. I just wanted to spend time with my mother. We enjoyed our meal together but then when I saw that she did not eat her food something really started to bother me.

At that same time, a family member was also struggling with childhood issues. When I shared this with my mom, she said it was time to tell us our whole family history. We all met at Applebee's again for a late lunch and Mom took us down a hard path.

She told us all about Bigma and the life she lived in the south. As my mother gave us the rundown of our matriarch's family history, I started to see a pattern: emotional and physical abuse, sexual addiction, alcoholism, and infidelity. It brought some understanding to what I had been dealing with for years. I prayed and asked God to help me process *everything* she told us. She spoke from her gut. It was painful to share all of the trauma she experienced as a young girl and even more painful for me to hear it. Yet, it didn't soften my feelings towards her, it just explained in part why she was who she was. I left that afternoon with more answers than I expected about myself. I wanted to go to the closet and write what I heard that day. I needed to unpack the feelings that were bubbling inside me about my family's history.

Abuse was prevalent throughout our family history; that's how everyone was kept in control. Control was the enemy's plan. If he could keep us in a life of discord, confusion, depression, and despair, then he could control our family's destiny. Something started to stir in me that I needed to confront this pattern of abuse and figure out how to stop it for the generations to come.

Digging into the health concern more, I found out that after an emergency room visit for what she believed was kidney stones, the ER doctor mentioned there was a spot seen on the diagnostics and it should be followed up with her doctor. Now, she was frail, and not eating as much. For her follow-up visit, I asked her to let me know what the doctor said. I even asked if I could go with her, which she said was not necessary.

A few weeks passed and we slowly began to get back to our once every two-day conversations even though I made sure not to keep her on the phone too long. Within myself I was still trying to hold boundaries. I was dealing with a lot of issues watching her give her life to this religious organization and diminish our relationship as mother and daughter. I knew I had to accept that this was going to be how our relationship would go. I was still dealing with the issues of my marriage as well.

One day she came to my job to tell me what her doctor said at her most recent visit. It had been a long day dealing with work tasks and missing staff, when my mom told me she was diagnosed with pancreatic cancer. One of her girlfriends, Crystal, went to the doctor's appointment with her when she was told this information. When they called her and asked her to come in they also asked her to bring someone with her to hear the news as well. Even though she didn't ask me, I was grateful it was a prayerful individual who was there to support her. When she sat in my office and told me the results I was absolutely stunned! She said she had told her pastor, and she was telling me, but no one else was to know. She said she would deal with this on her own and everything would be okay because she had assurance from God. There was no need for me to worry, she just felt it was necessary for me to know.

When she left, I immediately called my husband and told him what my mom said. His mom had passed away a little over a year prior, so we were still reeling from the loss and grief of losing a matriarch from my husband's side of the family and I wasn't ready to even consider that I was about to lose my mom. I made arrangements with my employer to be able to go to the doctor appointments that were coming up with my mom from that point on.

The first doctor's visit I attended with her was mind blowing! That was when I heard she was diagnosed with stage three pancreatic cancer and would need to start chemotherapy immediately. They explained the entire process of what was going to happen, and I still could not wrap my head around what was being said. Mom was very optimistic and understood that this was what she needed to do, but she felt that it was a distraction from what she wanted to do. What she wanted to do was to get out into the community and spread gospel tracts with her church congregation and serve the Lord in the way that they found appropriate. She wasn't going to let this keep her from doing God's will!

While she was getting blood work done, I had the opportunity to speak directly with her doctor to find out fully what was said during that first visit. Her doctor, a well-known oncologist, explained to me that the type of cancer that my mom had was aggressive and was going to be hard to fight. She would maybe live a year with the proper treatment, and she would need to gain weight in order to be able to handle the chemotherapy. He gave me his personal cell phone number just in case I had more questions because he knew this was going to be a battle that she was going to have to fight. He was a man of faith and believed strongly that her faith in God would bring her through this tough time. He also encouraged me that we needed to spend as much time as we could together and enjoy life as much as possible because of the type of cancer she had and where it was.

That's when I broke. I literally could not believe what I was hearing and immediately went into prayer asking God what He wanted me to do for my mommy and with her during this time. There was once a time when if you saw my mom, you saw me. Yet our lives were completely separate at this point because I was trying to focus on my marriage, giving it everything I had, and distancing myself from her. The issues I had been dealing with as a child were resurfacing as an adult. I found myself trying to hide it because once I pulled back from my mom, it was hard to ignore. My bouts of depression were becoming more frequent, and my husband and I had hit a hard patch in our marriage. I had been spending some time in the closet, crying, and praying for God to take away the darkness that was trying to engulf me again. What now? If I hide in the closet, I can't hear the phone ring. I can't hear her weak voice crying in pain, or fighting with me about the medication. I knew I had to come out of the closet but I felt like I was carrying the closet around with me at this point because I felt I had to be there for her as much as possible.

She didn't want anyone to know what was going on with her and at first, I respected her wishes.

She wore clothes that covered her chemo ports and evaded questions about her appearance. Because of my mom's position in the family, no one questioned her. In fact, many people were afraid of her, as they were with Bigma! I understood, because, I too, was afraid of my mother; afraid of her tongue lashing, her emotional withdrawal, her temperamental outbursts and her "godly" judgment. She would share much godly wisdom, but she could also whip out words that would cut me to my core. In an instance, it could take me back to being a kid and wanting only to please her so I could feel her love.

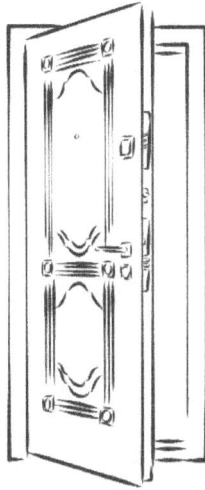

TWENTY-FIVE

B y this time, our younger children were graduating from high school. Darnell and I concluded that it was time to sell the house and move back to Detroit. The home was too big for the two of us and he was approximately five years away from retirement. We were still struggling in our marriage but managed to function as a couple. We wanted to do it for the sake of the kids. We didn't want them to experience a separation in their family unit while trying to finish high school.

We rented a beautiful rooftop two-bedroom apartment in downtown Detroit. It wasn't too far from the firehouse Darnell was assigned to and had a beautiful view of the Detroit River. We sold our home within two months of it going on the market and our youngest son, Kennon left for college in Louisiana. Our third child, Camille, was still living with us and attending community college for veterinary medicine. The older two children, Domenique, and Kortez were living on their own after finishing college.

As Momma's medical treatments started, I found myself taking over her personal finances and this was an eye-opening experience. She was broke. Her only income was her pension and social security which wasn't enough to maintain her current expenses. We moved her into an income-based senior building that was walking distance from the Detroit River and next door to where we lived. As word spread about her illness, people sent food, money, and resources to take care of her. It was amazing how God was providing for her every need; she was amazed at everyone's kindness. I was hearing God say, "Take care of her and I will take care of you."

It was a tough road those next twelve months because I took on the role as parent and caregiver, making sure that she had her medication, made it to her doctor's appointments, and sat with her and held her hand at night when the pain was too great. I would listen to her rant for all sorts of reasons. She still didn't want the family to know, but I could not keep it from them. The weight of what we were dealing with was great, and up until this point, I only had my husband and our youngest daughter to help me with this. I told my mom that I needed to tell Kenny and other family members about her diagnosis. She wasn't happy about it, but she didn't have a choice because at this point, she needed us there. Chemotherapy and radiation gave her some hope because the cancer started to diminish. There were moments of celebration for this. These moments provided hope that she would beat this thing and that she was not going to die. She even began to make plans for traveling and spending time with her family.

She continued her regimen of going to church and serving as the church secretary and treasurer, and when she could, she would go and pass out tracts. There came a point when she was too weak physically to continue on this path, but she did not let on to anyone else what she was dealing with. To them, she was beating this thing. Even though her body was weak, her voice was strong, and she seemed to be pushing through. When they left, we had to deal with the aftereffects of her expending all of her energy and strength to look strong for others.

I was tired of being strong and even using the word, "strong." Mom fought to maintain that appearance at almost any cost, and it caused her to eventually have to go into the hospital because of the lack of energy she had in her body. We had to rush her to the hospital, sit there in the emergency room, and wait patiently for them to find a hospital bed, only to hear them tell her she really needed to rest and that the cancer was progressing. She would often say, "I'll rest when I'm dead. I still have a lot to do." Her pastor would come by, and they would shout "Hallelujah" and praises of joy for what God was bringing her through and how "strong" she looked. I would ask him to please not get her so riled up, because when he left, we had to deal with the aftereffects. Without fail, she would become extremely weak. She would not complain about the pain while he was there because she believed that was a sign of weakness. Yet when he left, it was obvious that she was overdue for medication that would have headed-off the excruciating pain and nausea that she was about to endure. I specifically remember lying next to her and holding her frail little body close to mine; inside, dealing with all of these emotions. This woman whom I had learned to love, but had hated for so many years because of the treatment in my childhood, now in my arms, was dying of cancer. I struggled emotionally and spiritually within myself, battling hard to be her caregiver and also to be her daughter.

I'm certain my mother was sensing what I was feeling and the struggle I was dealing with. She would thank me and my husband for taking such good care of her. She would express her love and her appreciation for everything that we did for her as often as she could. She would hold my hand and talk to me about her life and the things that she dealt with down through the years. It was in those conversations, in those silent moments that we had together, that I began to see Lois Jean. I saw the little girl who many years ago was abused by her own mother and later by the men in her life. Little Lois Jean only wanted to be loved and give love. She loved the Lord so much and would sing His praises through everything she went through and in those moments she became my mother again, offering the love I longed for, for so many years. I received that love in those moments and embraced every second.

At this point, I had not completely embraced forgiveness, but it was definitely a work in progress within my heart. And every time I looked at her, I began to feel more and more compassion. I recorded some of our conversations and times with her while lying in bed. In these videos, I captured her smile as she repeated her love for me and my family. When I need to, I now watch these videos with tears of love. The sound of her voice brings me so much comfort; like a baby hearing their mom's voice, it soothes me.

I would pray and ask God to forgive me for the thoughts that were running through my head. Slowly, but surely, He changed the hurt and the hatred I had for her, to love and compassion for my mom. It went from doing caregiving tasks, to a service of love, to helping her through bath time, fixing her meals, and cleaning her house. It slowly, slowly changed from anger, to love, and compassion. And then at some point the joy of being her daughter was there. Now I'm not going to lie and say I didn't have my days when I just couldn't do it—there were hard days. Yet, looking back on it now, I would not change anything that we did together in those eighteen months. I was her advocate and her caregiver, but I was also her daughter and I realized just how much I loved this woman.

During her final visit in the hospital, just before Christmas 2017, she was demanding to know when she was starting her next round of chemotherapy. The doctors were trying in their own way to explain to her that the cancer had progressed and was now not only in her pancreas but also in her lungs and there was nothing else that they could do. She wasn't hearing it because God had assured her she was going to come through this. But I heard the words and that's when my grieving began. We were sent home with the instructions to enjoy the days that we have left. They could not tell her how much time she had. It could be three months, it could be six months, but we were advised to enjoy every moment. Her birthday was in six months, and I wanted to plan a nice little family gathering to celebrate her seventieth birthday. So we went home with the instructions to keep her comfortable.

The condition got worse quicker than we thought. Within thirty days of leaving the hospital, she was receiving hospice care at home. At first, she wouldn't entertain the thought of hospice. Finally, she was told that hospice would be a support for us to help take care of her and to keep her comfortable. She still would not tell anyone that she was at stage four. I felt like a traitor when I had to explain to people this *strong and mighty woman* was in her last days and that we were trying to just keep her comfortable. This was very hard emotionally and spiritually. I wanted so much for her to be healed completely physically and to enjoy life to the fullest but she was so locked into this religious life that she could not see. She couldn't enjoy the birds flying in the air, the smell of the Detroit River outside her bedroom door, or her family and friends who loved her dearly. In her head, everyone was out to get her.

Yet, as family began to come to visit, she finally realized just how much she was loved by so many in her life that she had shut out.

Her cousin Sherry, whom she had not connected with for some time, made sure to come and visit her on Saturdays to spend time with her. This gave me a break so that I could go and do some self-care, spend time with my husband and daughter, or just sleep. Her girlfriend Crystal, and Kenny, along with so many others gave us a break so they could spend time with her as well. She would often say, "I just did not know they felt that way about me." It broke my heart each time to hear that because she had closed herself off from everyone except her church family.

Hospice was a great help and supported us through the process. They helped us make the decision to send her to the hospital because of the amount of medication she was requiring every hour for the pain. I had to remind myself that it had been a horrendous eighteen-month process. My husband and I put our own issues on hold to take care of my mom. He took care of her as if she was his own mother while also maintaining our household so I could care for her. When we were told that she needed to go to the hospital for hospice care, he held me close because I knew she was close to the end.

The ambulance came to take her to the hospital, and we met her there. When we got there, they were preparing her in a room for intake and she was very erratic not understanding what was going on and I was trying to explain to her that she was in the hospital again and they were going to give her the care that she needed. Momma looked at my face and said, "I'm mad at you!" By this time, I was used to these types of conversations and I said, "Why Momma?" Then she said, "Because you took my baby from me!" Again, she looked me right in my eyes and said, "I'm mad at you, you took my baby from me." I didn't know what to make of it. I could not understand why she was so upset with me because we had tried to do everything that we could to take care of her, and up until this point she only expressed her appreciation, love, and undying dedication to my husband and I, and our daughter for providing care for her during this time. But she also thought she would physically be healed of this painful cancer. The nurse looked at me and said, "Don't take it personally. She is heavily medicated but she's going to be okay."

I later realized she was seeing her mother in me, because I had taken care of her as a mother would, but she still held anger towards her mother for making her abort her baby at age fifteen. She never forgot about that child she had to let go.

They needed to finish their intake and suggested that we go home and come back the next day. During the walk down the hallway I realized that I would never be able to talk to my mother again, to have her hugs, and her kisses, and love, because she was leaving. As much joy as I had in my heart that she would be on the other side one day soon looking at our Lord and Savior Jesus Christ, I also knew this would be the last time I could tell her I love her and hear her say "I love you too baby girl."

For the next eight days, she amazed everyone by hanging in there. The hospice nurse said she must be a strong-willed woman because she isn't going without a fight. All the family was called and told to come and say their last goodbyes if they wanted to, which they did. Every day, I stayed at the hospital because I wanted to be there. One evening I was so tired and exhausted I called the night nurse and asked them if they could put the phone to her ear so I could tell her that I wasn't coming that night. I told her how much I loved her, and that I would see her in the morning. Through the phone, I could hear the heavy breathing. She was still there.

The next morning my husband and I stopped for breakfast, had a cup of coffee, and then we made our way to her room. We met the morning nurse along the way who said that her vitals were the same and she was "so *strong.*" When we walked into the room, I did not hear her breathing. Her breath was very shallow and slow. The nurse took her vitals and looked up at us. She said, "the time has come." Her hand was still warm as I gripped it and I slowly began to tell her everything I wanted her to hear before her last breath. How proud I was of her, how much I loved her, and always would. I thanked her for being my mother, for giving me life, for teaching me to love the Lord with all my heart, body, soul and mind, and I thanked her for being such an amazing grandmother to our children. I also thanked her for waiting for me to get there before she left. My mom knew I would've wanted to be with her at that moment and usher her home to be with the Lord. I finally released my mom and told her we would be okay and that she could go. I told her that she didn't need to fight any longer, and that we would be fine. I said that we would remember everything she told us, and that we wanted her to be at peace. I repeated it over and over.

At last, she took her last breath as a single tear rolled down her face. She was gone. The tears fell down my face while I sat there holding her now chilled hand.

She was gone.

Last days with Momma.

The last time I held Momma's hand.

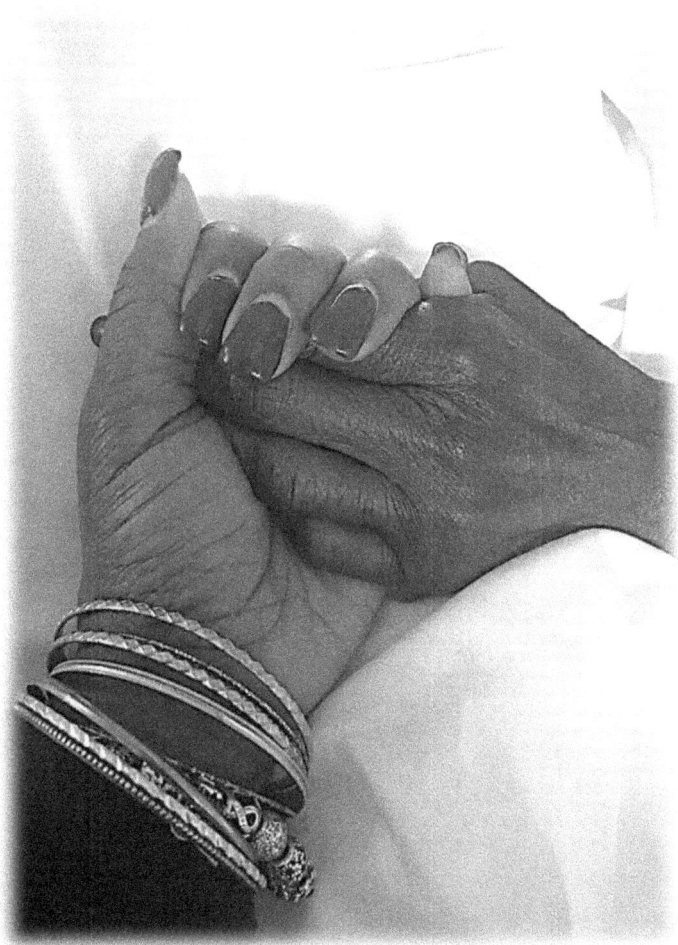

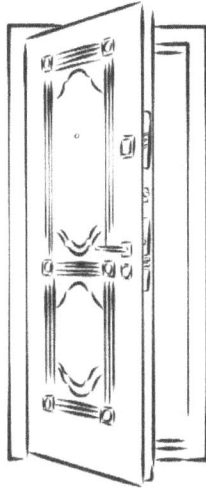

TWENTY–SIX

Darnell had kept his word that we would stay together, but it was a rocky few years, with him always wondering what I was doing, or if he could trust me, until one night when it all came to a head. By this time, we had moved from downtown Detroit to a home we owned on Detroit's west side. Camille moved out and was living on her own closer to the college she attended.

The emotional relationship that occurred had been over for approximately ten years, but to him it was as if it had just happened yesterday. In a very heated argument, I told him I could not take the mean-spirited words or the accusations anymore, and he said he couldn't take the thought of not knowing anymore. He needed the truth. That was when I knew I had to just let it all out; tell everything and not hold back. I had to give him the answers that he needed because he deserved it. Up to this point, I was so concerned about my own shame and guilt, walking in a selfish spirit, and not giving him the peace he needed. More importantly I was not trusting God to handle this entire situation. I had actually been praying to God to cover my indiscretion and to lie for me. In that moment of saying those words to my husband, oh, my voice quivered, a tear rolled down my cheek, and my body shook, but I knew I had to tell the truth. I couldn't hide behind the tears anymore or the lies. It all had to come out.

After I spoke those words of my full confession, a huge weight was lifted from my shoulders because it was all out now. The words came slow and intentional; I had to get it all out. Once I spoke the final words, I sat in silence waiting for his response and then came the tears and the words, "I knew it! I knew it!" He asked me if it was over and without a shadow of a doubt, I could answer that question with a strong yes! I asked him, "Where do we go from here?" I offered that I could sleep in the other room so that he could have time to process everything. His response was, "You sleep where you're most comfortable. I will never tell you not to come to our bed." I then said I would begin looking for some place else to go. Because in my mind, who would want to be with someone that has lied to them over and over and over again? Someone who had basically held you hostage by their own selfishness, instead of being honest? I stood in front of his face and lied to him. Oh, I honestly did not expect him to want to remain in this relationship anymore. The children were all gone. It was just me and him. We did not have to worry about the repercussions of our young children living in two households. I honestly thought that this was the end. That's just how much I allowed the lies and the enemy to penetrate my spirit.

I crossed the room and sat on the couch next to him sitting just close enough that we could barely touch but not to make any sudden moves. He stood up, put his hands out, helped me off the couch and hugged me. All of the anxiety, tears, fears, shame, and doubt came out. Released by my heaving sobs against his broad, comforting chest, I continued to say over and over again, "I'm so sorry I hurt you." He responded by whispering in my ear, "I love you. We've gotten through other stuff; we can get through this."

In that moment I felt an unbelievable presence of forgiveness. My husband fought for our marriage for so many years and it all came to a point in a matter of moments. He forgave me, and he never brought it up again. I could sit in that moment forever because it was God's redemption that I felt and the restoration of our marriage. That moment as we walked together hand-in-hand back upstairs to our bedroom, I kept thinking, is this what it feels like when God says He forgives us, and will never ever bring it up again? Is this the love, is this an example of the love our Father has for us, the unconditional love He has for His children? Is this agape love?

As we laid in bed that night his arms wrapped around my body I could not stop crying because of these thoughts going through my head or the thought that I caused him so much pain and hurt unnecessarily by not being honest.

We've gone through many ups and downs since then, but we both have been able to look at it from a different perspective. We can get through it together. I had to repent to God and ask Him to forgive me for the many prayers that I prayed asking for my indiscretions to be covered up. I asked for forgiveness for not being mindful of the priority our marriage should have had. I put so many other things before our marriage, before my husband, and now I understood God's plan. The husband *is* the head of our household and as a married couple *we had become one.* Up until this point I had not felt that we were one in our marriage. But, oh how that moment changed everything for us!

Darnell and I, 2021.

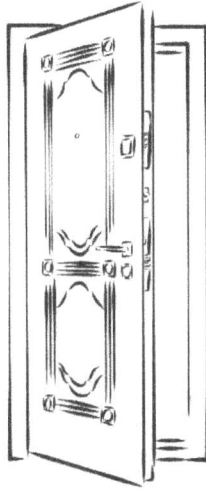

TWENTY–SEVEN

God never left me alone, even though there were many times through the years that I questioned if He was present. I didn't give my life to Christ until I was nine, but now looking back it doesn't surprise me that the enemy tried to take me out. He peaked into my future and saw the plans God had for my life. In a dream one night, the Holy Spirit showed me that I had angels standing around me, holding back the enemies that were commissioned against me. I realize now that I was being carried by God all my life.

Dealing with so much trauma in the early years of life helped me trust my gut and identify the dangers that were lurking. Yet my heightened sense of alertness turned into higher levels of anxiety that I couldn't control. The closet helped me hide from the outside dangers and bring down that level of anxiety, yet I didn't learn how to deal with life outside of it. Trina dealt in the moment and only found refuge in those places of shelter and solitude. Katrina needed to learn how to trust God for life and for covering.

Helen, the fortune teller, spoke truth about how my life would flourish. The three husbands she spoke of came to pass. Momma said the first husband was my oldest son's father, the second husband was the guy I was with before meeting the third and final husband. There would be no other man after him … he represented the happiness that would come. I won't say our life hasn't been filled with a lot of ups and downs, but we've learned to go through it together.

I had to learn how to be Darnell's wife, praying for God to teach me what my husband needed, and providing examples of marriages to look up to. The first was my paternal grandparents and aunts. They had only been married once, all of which lasted over forty years. Then there were marriages in the church where I worked. Some of those marriages lasted over fifty and sixty years. It gave me hope. I was blessed to be around other married women sharing life's experiences of real-life testimonies such as a husband coming to Christ after being on drugs for years, and another husband who refused to attend church but then who had an encounter with God that brought him into a relationship with Christ! I just had to keep believing God would heal our marriage and He did it!

Many people spoke life into me, but for a long time, I didn't believe it, I didn't receive it. It took years before I began to truly believe God's Word and plan for my life. I had to traverse many valleys; each one had a different lesson than the last. When I was paying attention, the lesson came with less scars, but when I wasn't attentive to God's voice, the lessons were more painful. Eventually, I learned how to listen to His voice, just as Jesus says in John 10:27, "My sheep listen to My voice; I know them and they follow Me." My closet experiences helped me to discern His voice from the voice of the enemy … Trina was fighting to protect me but Katrina had to learn to trust God and listen to His voice, so I, Katrina, could emerge.

Psalm 91 tells us that God is our protection and our refuge. He became my protection and refuge even though I couldn't see. He also became my redeemer because He took back the years of sorrow and turned them into stepping stones for His Glory. In 2 Timothy 2:12 it says, "If we endure hardship, we will reign with Him. If we deny Him, He will deny us." The Bible also says that our suffering is nothing compared to His. God continues to send young women into my life for love, mentoring, prayers, guidance, and motherly love. He used me to be the woman I needed when I was growing up.

I slowly came to a point where I could tell my story without trembling with fear, being triggered into an asthma attack, and crying all night in a deep depression. As I learned how to share my story, more of His Grace and Love embraced me through the people He placed in my life. He carried me through my entire life. Tears flow when I think of His goodness.

Some days I would cry out in painful desperation, "How could I face another day?" And He would respond:

"I already know what the day will bring because I created the day. You will rise above the storm like an eagle to soar above the clouds. You will know it was Me."

Hot tears rolled down my face that matched the heaviness in my heart.

Today, I cry tears of joy as I realize He could've let me go down that same road as Bigma, and Momma, but God said, "Katrina, you will share my Word through your testimony of My grace. People will look at you, the change in your life, and know it was Me. My Light will be evident in your life, speak My Truth. Your past will be a testimony of how I will give you beauty for your ashes. The struggle with Momma issues will be a testimony of redemptive power, compassion, and grace. Your marital issues are My path to show you My forgiving power and agape love. This pain will be a source of healing for you."

"How, it hurts so bad?" I cried.
"It's your story of My Grace." He replied.

It's endless. It's eternal. This was His promise to me in the closet all those years ago. It's my story of His everlasting grace. When it seemed impossible to get off the floor of the closet, He engulfed me in His worship. His angels ministered to my spirit, filling my broken soul with His love. He took my hand as I walked out of the closet while lifting my tear-stained face and wiping away the pain-filled tears.

Katrina Stewart

The closet was the cocoon for the change to manifest the blessing of this brown-toned soft beauty of a woman who He brought through trauma to grace. As I have finally written my story here, a flood of words filled my mind and my heart; words that speak to my spirit and confirm that I can continue to dream and see the vision of what is possible.

The dark cloud has lifted
The cloud of pain and hurt
The cloud of depression and defeat
The cloud of shame and doubt
The cloud of lies that were supposed to be my story …

The Light broke through to reveal the truth:

I am loved.
I am beautiful.
I am worthy.
I am strong.
Just like my momma.
I am capable.
I am gifted.
I am anointed.

The pain is a reminder.
The healing is a gift.
The story is a blessing.

God has done such an amazing thing in my life and I'm in awe of His goodness. As I read this story, I began to feel the release of the little girl … the release of Trina … the release of all the junk that has been sitting in the pit of my heart, of my stomach, of my soul. As I read this story, I can acknowledge it, but the pain …. it's not there … the healing has taken place. There is more healing yet to come, but the traumatized little girl is no longer here. Trina is not here anymore. By God's grace, Katrina wrote this story to help save others from the trauma that Trina went through so they can release that little girl too. God did it.

Do not be anxious about anything, but in everything by prayer and supplication with thanksgiving let your requests be made known to God. And the peace of God, which surpasses all understanding, will guard your hearts and your minds in Christ Jesus.
Philippians 4:6-7 ESV

You keep him in perfect peace
whose mind is stayed on you,
because he trusts in you.
Isaiah 26:3 ESV

God is in the midst of her; she shall not be moved;
God will help her when morning dawns.
Psalm 46:5 ESV

ABOUT THE AUTHOR: KATRINA STEWART

Katrina Stewart has been an author at heart for many years; finally publishing her first book, *Through Trauma to Grace*.

Katrina is a graduate of Rochester University where she studied Early Childhood Development. It was through this Christian learning environment where she began to focus on brain development, psychology, and more specifically how childhood experiences can affect an individual's adulthood. These fueled Katrina's desire to always know the why behind many actions and later inspired her to focus on the generational trauma that plagued her family.

Her passion has always evolved around evangelism within women's ministry, where she can share her life experiences and be the person she needed when she was growing up.

Most importantly, she is wife to Darnell, mom to four beautiful adult children and grandma to a rambunctious grandson.

Katrina's books are available on Amazon.com and BarnesandNoble.com.

Connect with Katrina:
stewconsultllc@gmail.com

Additional copies of this book
may be purchased
on Amazon.com
and BarnesandNoble.com

www.ingramcontent.com/pod-product-compliance
Lightning Source LLC
LaVergne TN
LVHW011324080426
835513LV00006B/188